THE
UNCONSCIOUS
CONSPIRACY

Why Leaders Can't Lead

WARREN G. BENNIS

THE
UNCONSCIOUS
CONSPIRACY
Why Leaders Can't Lead

A DIVISION OF AMERICAN MANAGEMENT ASSOCIATIONS

Library of Congress Cataloging in Publication Data

Bennis, Warren G
 The unconscious conspiracy.

 1. Leadership. 2. Social change. 3. Civiliza-
tion, Modern--20th century. 4. United States--
Civilization. I. Title.
HM141.B43   301.15'53   75-37851
ISBN 0-8144-5406-2

Second Printing

FOREWORD

Why? Or How come?

Anyone who knows Warren Bennis can identify these questions as the ones he is most likely to ask. Curiosity that is scholarly, objective, probing—free of cynicism, prying, or belittling—is one among his many great characteristics. The result of his questioning is a book such as this.

Like everyone else, he is worried by the lack of leaders and the loss of leadership in the world. We are all hard pressed to name one great statesman in any country today. Is there a church leader with the unqualified respect of all faiths? Is there an outstanding educator? Pose the same question about the corporate world, science, and politics. The absence of a ready answer brings the rejoinder, "If there were one, the name would be on your lips."

Warren Bennis, in his usual inquiring fashion, is joining the quest in this book. But do not expect answers. The great contribution we find here is analysis, a digging into the nature of contemporary society to find out why would-be leaders—people who are in positions that permit, if not demand, leadership—are frustrated in their efforts and cynical about how the society may receive, distort, or subvert their initiatives. Moreover, their visibility, which has always made them vulnerable, has been intensified by the media so

v

that the errors they make are not allowed to pass unnoticed and be rectified before a reputation can be harmed or confidence undermined. Bennis makes us take a hard look at the ways in which we have shaped our present society to make all this inevitable. But his characteristic approach, which warmly reflects his great empathy for people in difficult jobs, makes us feel wistful as well as angry.

It was "Democracy Is Inevitable" that caught my eye in 1964 in the *Harvard Business Review*. Back then Bennis was saying that "leadership is as much craft as science. . . . The main instrument or tool for the leader-as-craftsman is himself." In the years since then, as he moved from the role of educator to administrator, his experience engendered greater pragmatism, and so in *The Leaning Ivory Tower* he described leadership as "the capacity to infuse new values and goals into the organization, to provide perspective on events and environments which, if unnoticed, can impose constraints on the institution." Note the change from a method to a capacity, from a set of isolated conditions to an environment. Now we need to examine that environment to find out why it has stultified leaders everywhere.

This is the strength of Warren Bennis—continuous growth with every new experience. Answering the question of Why? or How come? has produced this most interesting book.

JAMES L. HAYES, *President*
American Management Associations

vi

PREFACE

In the whirl and swirl of these years of our days—particularly the six years since 1970 when these collected commentaries and articles were first written—so much has turned topsy-turvy in our lives that the only thing predictable seems to be the unpredictable. Well might we rewrite the aphorism: *plus ça change, plus ça change.*

The only unchanging constant is change, and even "the changing scale and scope of change itself," as Robert Oppenheimer observed, is such "that the world alters even as we walk on it." A decade ago, had I gone around saying "I have a colleague who walked on the moon," I might have been put away. Today I can propose Neil Armstrong to the Cincinnati Rotary Club, supposedly limited to one member per category, and suggest a new one—"Moon walker"—without raising more than a chuckle.

Change has been so swift since 1970, the concatenation of unexpectable events so accelerated, that it would be remarkable if observations written over this span were not often overrun by events. When, for example, in 1972, I suggested (in *Resignation for Principle*) that a leader can sometimes serve best by departing, I could scarcely have anticipated that within two years, for the first time in history, a President of the United States would be forced to resign—not from principle but from necessity.

Accordingly, the observations in this book, while essentially unchanged from the original, have been edited to take note of facts and events that occurred subsequent to their publication. The conclusions remain valid, I trust.

All have a single theme: leadership. Their common assumption is that all leaders, of all large organizations, face basically the same problems. These problems grow ever more complex even as the leader's own authority and autonomy grow more circumscribed by events and forces often beyond his or her control.

These commentaries raise more questions than they offer answers. Indeed, they recognize that many problems have only *proximate* solutions, and that some, in an era now recognizing the limits of both military power and the vaunted miracles of technology, must simply be marked "NTS"—no technical solution.

The commentaries seek to distinguish true leadership from mere managing, however brilliant the managing may be, and show the difference. They ask why it is that today's leaders, from the President down, seemingly cannot lead. In a time when the only leaders the young respect are dead, they ask: "Where have all the leaders gone?"

The answers will not be easily found. It can only be hoped that the questions raised here will help to stimulate today's leaders to ask still more searching questions.

As one who has been challenged to be, and strives his often-frustrated best to become, a leader, the writer is as torn, troubled, fragmented, harried, and frequently baffled as any of his fellows. He is still optimist enough to believe that asking the right questions can sometimes—*sometimes*—lead toward the right answers. Herein, however uncertainly or tentatively, he attempts that.

WARREN BENNIS

CONTENTS

ORDEAL BY LEADERSHIP
One Job, One Year, One Life   3
The Unconscious Conspiracy—
and How to Confound It   18

THE OPTIONS
Resignation for Principle   37
Surviving the Revolution of Consciousness   55

THE IMAGE AND THE REALITIES
A Little Lower than the Angels   71
People, Change, and the Adaptive Process   84
Perils of the Bureaucratic Way   101
Meet Me in Macy's Window   114
Leader Power in an Explosive Environment   125

"MORTAL STAKES"
Where Have All the Leaders Gone?   143
The Shape of the Future   157

Acknowledgments   179

ORDEAL
BY LEADERSHIP

But hard it is to learn the mind of any mortal, or the heart, till he be tried in chief authority. Power shows the man.

Sophocles, *Antigone*

ONE JOB, ONE YEAR, ONE LIFE

On June 17, 1969, at 8:20 A.M., one day after his last "ordeal" as acting president of the University of Oregon, Dr. Charles Johnson rounded a sharp, blind curve and drove his Volkswagen head-on into a Mack B-61 diesel log truck and Peerless log trailer with a load of 13 logs weighing 16 tons. The total weight was around 36 tons. Johnson died instantly. He was 48.

Johnson's body was so mutilated not even his closest associates could identify him with certainty. Many thought he had committed suicide. They said:

"He was depressed."
"Everybody knows it."
"I heard it on the radio."
"Just ask anybody."
"He always took the easy way out. He always caved in to student demands. His suicide was just one more easy way out."

James Jensen, the president of Oregon State University, said something else: "This is a terrible tragedy. I hope now the people of Oregon will understand. . . ."

He paused.

"Well, perhaps I'd just better not say what I hope the people of Oregon will understand."

The county medical investigator ruled the death an accident. The curve was a difficult turn that had to be made very carefully, and the sun had been in Johnson's eyes. A psychiatrist who had seen Johnson several days before felt that it was "partial dissociation," "a situational depression caused possibly by some recent campus crisis." Johnson was also weak from a recent bout with Asian flu. And he was known to be an erratic driver.

All that we know with any certainty is that many in Oregon, and especially those connected with the University of Oregon, shared after the fact a morbid sense of collective guilt.

In 1973, four years after the death of Dr. Johnson, Ken Metzler published a book entitled *Confrontation: The Destruction of a College President.** This book is a faithful chronicle of one year in the life of a university president. Ken Metzler is an associate professor of journalism at the University of Oregon and editor of its alumni magazine. Metzler also served as a secretary to the presidential search committee, which, six weeks before the Acting President's death, after excruciatingly intense and erratic deliberations, finally passed over this favorite of many to choose a former University of Oregon dean, Robert D. Clark, then president of San Jose State.

Reading the book some years away from the acrid stench of the Kent State and Jackson State tragedies is an eerie experience. The problems now facing higher education seem so different, so businesslike—they are concerned with "fiscal viability," "affirmative action," even with stu-

* Nash Publishing Corporation, Los Angeles.

4

dent apathy and other penultimate questions such as "Who benefits from higher education?" and "Who should pay for it?" Today college presidents are concerned about the relationship between jobs and education, about growing parsimony at the federal and state levels, and about ways to balance the books. They wince at the memory of the unsystematic growth of the 1950s and 1960s when most universities (the University of Oregon is a brilliant and bittersweet example) grew and grew like Topsy, proliferating their functions, diffusing their purposes, just doing what came naturally during the two golden decades: operating on margin very like 1929's speculators—hiring four professors on "soft money" (federally supported grants) to one on "hard money" (from general funds). They see graduate education, the indicator of a university's prestige, seriously jeopardized not only by fewer funds (a 40 percent dip in federal fellowships in the sciences alone between 1970 and 1973) but also by fewer students and, worse, fewer jobs. For every four graduate PhD's in the two decades between 1950 and 1969, three found positions with expanding or new campuses while only one replaced a professor who had died or retired.* Four years later, in many academic areas, only *one* of four graduating PhD's would find a job in what he or she was trained for, research and teaching in a university.

The problems Acting President Johnson faced in his year may seem quaint in retrospect; in fact, they were killers. Johnson had to deal in rapid succession with—

- An anemic version of the free-speech movement, which took form in an outcry about the use of obscenities in the student newspaper.

* See the 1973 *Newman Report on Graduate Education.*

5

- A confrontation between two black basketball players who refused to cut their Afros and a new and promising freshman coach who had ordered them to do so, culminating in a demonstration with serious possibilities of violent disruption.
- A dispute concerning the use of California table grapes in the University of Oregon dining halls.
- Other "brush fires" (Johnson's term) dealing with black students' rights, the bombing and destruction of valuable and expensive ROTC equipment, and similar problems which then convulsed our fragile institutions of higher learning.

Dr. Johnson also inherited a messy fiscal situation from his predecessor, the ebullient former HEW Secretary Arthur Flemming, who ran the university for the seven years preceding Johnson's term of office with a "go-go" style of enthusiasm, optimism, and "devil take the hindmost." Flemming employed a "management by addition" style of leadership, one followed by many public institutions and some private ones in those beamish years in an attempt to compete with the Eastern educational establishment.

Dr. Johnson comes through as an unpretentious, wry man of dry wit, strong analytic powers, and self-effacing style. He was healthily skeptical of power but at times wanted it more than his words—especially his letters to the folks back home—can conceal. He was straightforward, awkward, homespun. He enjoyed parlor games and rural jokes, he liked spending time with his family, and, most of all, he enjoyed good fun.

He was also almost totally inaccessible to his own feelings—and, in turn, to other people's feelings. I doubt that

Dr. Johnson and his family would ever term him complex, but complex he was, and especially so as to whatever tragic flaw held him in its vise and then slowly released him.

Whatever issue popped up on or careened off the University of Oregon campus in the 1968–1969 academic year, Dr. Johnson was usually in the middle of it. In the obscenity issue he was hit with the fallout of the "moderate liberal" reputation of that "highfalutin' and gallivantin' politician" Arthur Flemming and was able to secure the respect of at least some members of the academic community by standing on the venerable principle of free speech. The "hair" issue found him optimistically trying somehow to convince the coach to relax his rules or the players to shave off perhaps not the *whole* Afro but possibly an inch or two. Here he was caught in the middle of a "no win" situation. He took the side of the two black players. The promising young coach was ordered to stay home rather than be at the game, and to make matters worse the team lost badly. The sports and editorial writers, alumni, public officials, citizenry, and legislators (these last then in session determining the University's budget) were incensed and outraged.

Then there was the grape issue. Cesar Chavez's attempts to unionize the migrant grape pickers in California captivated some students who "demanded" the university boycott non-UFL (United Farm Labor) grapes. When the case first came up, earlier in the year, Johnson had to ask his daughter, a UO freshman, who Chavez was and what this was all about. Later in the year he publicly called a halt to the purchasing of grapes for reasons that had very little to do with the grape boycott. In so doing, he infuriated some legislators who were directly involved in marketing grapes.

Dr. Johnson sought valiantly to uphold the classic self-concept of the American university as a citadel of contemplation sheltering all hostages of a "sick society," defending the bastions of ideas against Philistine outrages. In fact, such confrontations make the vaunted bastion appear like little more than the flimsiest scrim, pitifully vulnerable to pot shots from the neighboring community. The alumni, the press, the legislators, the general public, the parents, and all those concerned with the support of the university, through either alumni giving or taxes, escalated their attacks against it. One could wish to report there was appreciation and generosity within the University for Johnson's courageous stands, but more often than not, apart from an infrequent pat on the back or an occasional faculty letter commending his principles, the internal "community" was mute or even "annoyed." The dissatisfactions that enraged the citizenry were far more strident, shrill, and incessant than could ever be counterbalanced by whatever satisfactions Johnson's decisions had meant for the academic community.

In any case the point should not be missed: *Universities have become more and more permeable to outside forces* and hence "politicized." One reason is that the proliferation and diffusion of goals *away* from teaching and learning and relatively more into public service and sponsored research inevitably shrink the relative autonomy of university organizations. This is not to say that universities should not undertake responsibilities for public service or contracts with external sponsors. But, when one increases rapidly the number of obligations external to research and teaching, it is inevitable that responsibilities are at the very least expanded and at the worst may be in conflict with the pivotal mission of the university.

Moreover, while universities manage and control extraordinary resources, human, financial, and physical, they are *not* self-supporting. Unlike many other institutions, universities are dependent upon tuition and gifts and alumni contributions, as well as taxpayers in the case of the major public institutions (which today have 80 percent of the students enrolled in higher education versus 50 percent in 1955).

Paradoxically, while there is no institution more vulnerable to, and hence more dependent on, external forces than the American university, its faculty, students, and administrators tend to ignore or deny these forces. Their self-image is still related to the medieval concept of the walled city, or the reclusive air of Oxbridge where the mundane problems of life are several terrain features away from the life of the mind. What is needed, organizationally speaking, between what Claude Bernard, the great French physiologist, called the *milieu intérieur* and the *milieu extérieur*, is a delicate balance providing enough autonomy for the inside to be protected from the momentary fads, political vagaries, and financial vicissitudes of the outside, and at the same time a system open enough for the outside indeed to have a *selective* permeability. The falsely lulling self-image that the university is remote and distant and somewhat "above" the society that nourishes and feeds it is not only outdated but one that, if believed and acted on, will bring about the university's destruction.

The "outside" clobbered Johnson. While he seemed aware of its stings and fangs, he refused to fully understand their impact on him and his future. Indeed, it was the outside, not the favorably disposed inside, that caused Johnson's rejection as the permanent president; it was the outside that led to his demise.

What happened that was so serious as to fundamentally alter Johnson's effectiveness and personality? What happened to this thoughtful and high-principled, liberal, and, above all, decent human being? What mysterious thing seemed to intervene between his own knowledge of the situation and his action? He was so perceptive, so aware of those forces which could destroy him, yet something disarmed his intellectual mastery before a wise, practical judgment could be made.

He said early that he would help to avoid confrontations between "highly polarized groups which see each other as adversaries to be defeated rather than as responsible partners engaged in a search for better ways of attaining mutually desired objectives." Good liberal talk. Thoughtful. Aware. A disaster in practice. What happened?

Ken Metzler conducted more than 300 interviews, talking to many of Johnson's close friends and relatives. He was fortunate to have in his subject a man who himself faithfully recorded his ideas and his premonitions and described his own behavior and decisions. Thus we have access to the raw experiences of *a man in crisis*. This allows us to employ a variety of analytic prisms in seeking to explain at least some of the man's behavior and the events that occurred. The prisms we use prefigure our analysis. I shall attempt to employ a few to determine my own focus of convenience.

So what went wrong?

Perhaps the most obvious fact is that Johnson had "psychological problems." He had suffered a number of serious lapses referred to by his own psychiatrist as "dissociative processes" and, specifically, an attack of "fugue" in which shortly before his death he had driven two miles one night, wandered dazed in the woods and, once, into a river without seeming to know what he had done. This seemed to be partly induced by overwork, by weakness from his attack of the flu, and doubtless also by shock and despair over having been passed over—despite his claimed disinterest in the job.

Johnson's childhood included the early death of his mother and obvious problems of achievement; somehow he often managed to *just miss* his goal ever so slightly. Thus, in military school, his height enabled him to make the basketball team, but he spent most of the season on the bench, dejected, head down, until he finally gave it up. He was very interested in the Scouts and attained the near-top status of Life Scout but stopped just *one* merit badge short of No. 1 rank, Eagle Scout. Lofty and strong ambition shows through the self-depreciation of his awkward posture of gawkiness (he was 6 feet 4 inches tall) and rural "plain folks" humor. He seems forever ambling backward, but always upward. His letters to his parents were painfully revealing: "Oh, I guess I might allow my name to be forwarded to the search committee, although the classroom sure does beckon; teaching is simplicity and I love it. But, still, maybe they'll be 'dumb enough' to accept this old country boy." So his country-boy manner, partly real, partly feigned, was an effective mask to grope backward and upward without ever looking too bad if he fell in the process. (If you fall in the process, then at least it is not altogether visible and people will think you are just fooling anyway.)

He was a man who embodied the core values of the academy and its institutional imperative, cognitive *rationality:* the life of the mind, inexorable logic, reliance on numbers and verbal symbols as strategies of truth (for a man who was a CPA by background and a professor of accounting, it was primarily numbers). This was the very basis of reality for Johnson.

The rationality was confronted in the "hair" episode, with irrational, strident voices from outside who rhetoricized its issues in such emotional terms as "knuckling under to those 'colored' folks." How could he respond to letters from all of the "concerned" citizens who questioned his patriotism and attacked him for his "lack" of firmness, backbone, and discipline? How does one use logic, empiricism, and the fact finding of the democratic process—slow, creaky, and painfully banal in its operation—to compete with the aphrodisia of confrontations where the operative slogan of the most destructive student radicals could be summarized as "Act now, think later!" and where the highest level of dialog to meet Johnson's lengthy, patient, and painstakingly clear explanations was a terse and reflexive "Bullshit!"?

Perhaps all this psychologizing is irrelevant. Metzler says Johnson was "the wrong man for the wrong job at the wrong time." Perhaps it was the Peter Principle at work —and Johnson's former experience as dean of a college not only did not prepare him for the presidency but might have instilled in him certain principles and guidelines to action which were antithetical to the pneumatic beat of the crises that were continually hammered out on the anvil of Johnson's psyche. Beneath his humility was a driving, perfectionist ambition, spurred perhaps by a demanding and puritanical father, a kind of No. 2 syndrome, and considerable grief and loneliness, while young, because of his gangling awkwardness.

Perhaps it was the times. Who in the world in a top position at any major university could have successfully coped with the exquisite pains and pressures of that year of 1968–1969? In every single case there was *no way* that Johnson could have planted even a small flag of victory. The best he could do in situation after situation was to *minimize* damage or danger or loss. And these terrible little, irrational brushfires continually interfered with what this accounting professor knew to be, long before others throughout the country suspected it, a terrible financial overextension of the university. Hoping to reverse it, he would retire to his home any nights that he could stay away from his demanding social obligations and, taking his budget to the bedroom, work on it, night after night, alone.

Having lived through that period as an administrator, I find it impossible to second-guess anybody's decisions during that chaotic time. Who will ever know, despite Metzler's minute detail, the existential moment of truth that Johnson had to face? In his commencement talk Johnson concluded with Dickens's "It was the best of times, it was the worst of times . . . ." For those who were in Johnson's shoes in that final year of a decade which started off so beautifully for higher education and ended up so ravaged, one could only say that it was the worst of times.

Perhaps it was Johnson's leadership style. My guess is that it was the "liberal" administrator who had the roughest time during that ordeal. The liberal presidents who began office then included Kenneth Pitzer of Stanford, Morris Abram of Brandeis, Robert Etherington of Wesleyan; all resigned before their second year. I suspect the trouble is in the liberal style—a style of negotiation, of splitting differences, of bringing people together to iron out differences, a tendency to banish differences, of sitting down with the coach and the black players and "talking it out." This style could work during times of shared values, but not in the charged and polarized situation that developed then. It is one thing to negotiate differences when the stakes are currency or economic gain, the kinds of things labor union and management bring to the table. It is another thing to negotiate between morally antithetical viewpoints.

Wanting to demonstrate how the poor had to live, that spring some students started moving old tar paper shacks onto the front of the beautiful campus lawn. Daily, more and more shacks appeared. How many, if any, should be allowed? Do you ask the students to remove all the shacks but, say, one (in order to demonstrate and amplify the meaning of poverty) and, for that, offer to provide them more courses in social justice, poverty, and "peaceful or nonviolent means of social change"?

Often Johnson seemed to walk into situations with the belief that he personally could get the two sides or the three sides to reason together into some viable consensus. But how could one bring about reason—much less consensus— between and among an outraged citizenry, black students striving for their own group identity and consciousness, the sons and daughters of mechanics and farmers who were spending their last dollar to send their children to school, alumni acutely concerned with the slippage of Oregon's athletic programs, and a faculty devoted to making the University of Oregon competitive with elite universities? At the same time, another President Johnson was discovering that Isaiah's wisdom could reach neither Hanoi, Saigon, nor the SDS.

From the analytic prism of a student of organizational behavior, I would say that the university's social organization doesn't provide the adjustive mechanisms of protection and cushioning for the president. It is simply ridiculous to think that the president of a major American corporation would be involved in some of the situations that Johnson found himself in—and that, occasionally, I find myself in. Yet corporation presidents and chairmen, like the chief executives of all our institutions, have equivalent nightmares.

An industrial case in point—if, indeed, one is needed—is the story of Eli M. Black, who at 8 A.M. on February 3, 1975, at the age of 53, plunged to his death from the 44th floor of New York's Pan Am Building. Both doors to his office were found bolted from the inside, according to detectives, and a sealed quarter-inch tempered plate glass window had been smashed open—apparently with Black's attaché case.

Black had been chairman of the United Brands Company, a conglomerate which he personally built from a small firm making milk-bottle caps to the point where it could take over, first, one of the country's largest meat packers (John Morrell & Co.), and, second, the United Fruit Company. United Brands, said *The New York Times*, had incurred heavy losses in Central American banana plantations from Hurricane Fifi, had undergone new burdens with export taxes on bananas imposed by Central American republics, and had sustained losses in its meat-packing division as a result of increased costs of feeding cattle. Black family members and business associates suggested that additional business pressures—mainly those connected with the sale of Foster Grant—were responsible for Black's state of mind, which was "low."

A subsequent investigation by the Securities and Exchange Commission, routinely conducted after the suicide of any top corporate executive, turned up another possible reason for Black's decision to take his life. According to *Newsweek* (April 21, 1975), the SEC inquiry disclosed that Black had authorized the payment of more than $2 million to government officials in Honduras to obtain a tax reduction on the export of bananas. Moreover, the facts seem to indicate that he must have known of other instances of bribery on the part of the big multinational company during his tenure.

Black's closest associates, who knew him as a man who put in mercilessly long hours and spent his limited free time working for various Jewish philanthropies, said that he had been determined to end United's image as a Yankee exploiter. If Black did approve the bribes, they insisted, he must have been under heavy pressure to do so.

What happens to top men—and I think that men and women who are *new* to the burdens of high position are especially vulnerable because they are trying to prove themselves—is that they end up with a kind of battle fatigue, overworked, acting as policemen and/or ombudsmen and, what's worse, seriously undermining the legitimacy and effectiveness of the other executives reporting to them. They tend to intervene compulsively, arrogating from loyal and competent subordinates what rightly belongs to them. Presidents can become burnt-out victims of the Peter Principle while denying the best potential leaders below them the responsibility needed for their own learning and development.

Finally, and most of all, we have to question seriously how much caring all of us can develop for our institutions when, at this historical time, they are becoming the anvil and test of all our society's crises and problems. The universities were perhaps the first to feel the real crunch. Metzler says that the problem with Johnson was that "he cared too much for the institution." Though it may have seemed that way, I don't think it is "caring too much" when one identifies his own self-esteem with the success of the institution. This in fact causes men to identify so much with their institution that they become indivisible with it, so that a rock thrown by an angry student through a window is morally and psychologically identical with the physical hurt of the president, so that the success of the football team against its chief rival is related to how one feels about one's own success. To care about an institution means to create a self-activating life, a life of its own, where there is a possibility for others to understand it and care for it and to care for the men and women who are attempting against difficult odds to make their work have meaning in a humane and democratic manner.

The problem is this: How do we develop a sufficient climate of understanding where the various publics on whom every present-day institution depends for its support, both financial and moral, as well as the people who take its classes or work in its plants and offices, care about the institution and identify with its destiny? Only then will the "best and the brightest" manage to succeed. Without caring, who cares? The institution wouldn't be a place that any of us would like to be responsible for or preside over anyway.

The threads of legitimacy and responsible authority fray too easily and far too rapidly. American universities underwent a very specific and unusual year, but it would be wrong to think that the lessons they learned the hard way apply only to the academy and to a receding period of past history. They apply to all time and all people and institutions and the fury of the fates that determine their destiny.

THE UNCONSCIOUS
CONSPIRACY-AND HOW
TO CONFOUND IT

BEFORE Clark Kerr went through the revolving presidential door at Berkeley, he defined the modern multiversity president's job. It was, he said, to provide "sex for the students, football for the alumni, and parking for the faculty." Eight years later, after my own maiden year as president of the University of Cincinnati—whose 36,104 students make it the largest urban multiversity in the country after New York City's—I can report:

* The parking problem is worse.
* College football is being energetically chased by man-eating tigers (in our case the Bengals).
* Sex is so taken for granted as to rate no priority.

If the problems change, however, they grow no fewer. All of them, whether from outside the university or from within it, no matter how trivial or irrelevant, wind up on the president's desk. Throughout my first year, the mere job of clearing it often kept me there until the small hours —far longer than what I accomplished seemed to justify. I appreciated more than ever the pertinence of Herman B.

Wells's observation, after leaving Indiana's presidency, that a college president should be born with "the physical stamina of a Greek athlete, the cunning of a Machiavelli, the wisdom of a Solomon, the courage of a lion if possible," but, above all, "the stomach of a goat."

As, goatlike, I chew the ruminative cud of that first year's academic detritus, I think I begin to understand why so many first-class men, often the finest and the best, decide to quit the presidential chair before they have scarcely warmed it, staying in some cases less time than it took the search committee to find them.

My moment of truth came toward the end of my first ten months. It was one of those nights in the office. The clock was moving toward four in the morning, and I was still not through with the incredible mass of paper stacked before me. I was bone-weary and soul-weary, and I found myself muttering, "Either I can't manage this place, or it's unmanageable." I reached for my calendar and ran my eyes down each hour, half-hour, quarter-hour, to see where my time had gone that day, the day before, the month before.

Nobel laureate James Franck has said he always recognizes a moment of discovery by "the feeling of terror that seizes me." I felt a trace of it that morning. My discovery was this: *I had become the victim of a vast, amorphous, unwitting, unconscious conspiracy to prevent me from doing anything whatever to change the university's status quo.* Even those of my associates who fully shared my hopes to set new goals, new directions, to work toward creative change were unconsciously often doing the most to make sure that I would never find the time to begin. I found myself thinking of a friend and former colleague who had taken over one of our top universities with goals and plans that fired up all those around him and who said when he left a few years later: "I never could get around to doing the things I wanted to do."

This discovery, or rediscovery, has led me to formulate what might be called Bennis's First Law of Academic Pseudodynamics, to wit: Routine work drives out nonroutine work, or: how to smother to death all creative planning, all fundamental change in the university—or *any* institution.

This insight also gave me the strength I needed to get through the year. All my academic training and a great deal of its practical application as a consultant to business and other organizations had concerned the rational development of managerial strengths and the tactics and strategy for their optimal use. Now I was being confronted with the acid test: whether I, as a "leading theorist" of the principles of creative leadership, actually could prove myself a leader. I resolved that in the year ahead I would either do so or confess that I had better go back to the classroom to develop some better theory.

But, first, some illustrations of the First Law. To start, there are 150 letters in the day's mail that require a response. About 50 of them concern our young dean of the School of Education, Hendrik Gideonse. Gideonse's job is to bring about change in the teaching of teachers, in our university's relationship to the public schools and to students in the deprived and deteriorating neighborhood around us. Out of these urban schools will come the bulk of our students of the future—as good or as bad as the schools have shaped them.

But the letters. They're not about education—they're about a baby, the dean's ten-week-old son. Gideonse feels very strongly about certain basic values. He feels especially so about sex roles, about equality for his wife, about making sure she has the time and freedom to develop her own potentials fully. So he's been carrying the baby into his office two days a week in a little bassinet, keeping him on his desk while he does his work. The daily *Enquirer* heard about all this, took a picture of Hendrik, baby, and bassinet, and played it on page one. TV splashed it across the nation —and my "in" basket has been overflowing ever since with letters that urge his arrest or merely his immediate dismissal. My only public comment has been that we're a tax-supported institution and, if Hendrik can engage in this form of applied humanism and still accomplish the things we both want done in education, then, like Lincoln with Grant's whiskey, I'd gladly send him several new babies for adoption. Nevertheless, Hendrik's baby is eating up quite a bit of my time.

Here's a note from a professor, complaining that his classroom temperature is down to 65 degrees: I suppose he expects me to grab a wrench and fix it. A student complains we won't give him course credit for acting as assistant to a city councilman. Another was unable to get into the student health center. The teacher at my child's day school, who goes to UC, is dissatisfied with her grades. A parent complains about four-letter words in a Philip Roth book being used in an English class. The track coach wants me to come over to see for myself how bad the track is. An alumnus couldn't get the football seat he wanted. Another wants a coach fired. A teacher just called to tell me the squash court was closed at 7 P.M., when he wanted to use it.

Last year perhaps 20 percent of my time was taken up by a problem at the General Hospital. It is city-owned but is administered by the University and serves as the teaching hospital of our medical school. Some terminal-cancer patients, with their consent, had been subjected to whole-body radiation as possibly beneficial therapy. Since the

Pentagon saw this as a convenient way to gather data that might help protect civilian population in nuclear warfare, it provided a series of subsidies for the work.

When this story broke and was pursued in such a way as to call up comparisons with the Nazis' experiments on human guinea pigs, it became almost impossible for me or anybody else to separate the essential facts from the fantasized distortions. The problem, I hope, has subsided (after a blue-ribbon task force recommended significant changes in the experiment's design). But I have also invested endless time in a matter only vaguely related to the prime purposes of our university—and wound up being accused by some of interfering with academic freedom. Together with the story of Hendrik's baby, the episode illustrates how the media, particularly TV, make the academic cloister a global village in a goldfish bowl. By focusing on the lurid or the superficial, they can disrupt a president's proper activities while contributing nothing to the advancement of knowledge.

This leads me to Bennis's Second Law of Academic Pseudodynamics: Make whatever grand plans you will, you may be sure the unexpected or the trivial will disturb and disrupt them.

What "grand plans"—what fundamental change, what creative reshaping of the goals and purposes—should I (and other presidents) be making? In order to see where we are going, it may be helpful, as Lincoln suggested, to see first where we are.

Higher education is now at a great historic watershed— what Clark Kerr has aptly called Climacteric II. The first climacteric was that great period of growth between 1870 and 1900, following on the Morrill Act and the establishment of land-grant colleges. But the growth following

World War II was simply staggering. The wartime baby boom flooded campuses with an ever increasing influx of students. Blank checks from federal and other subsidies flooded them with seemingly limitless resources for expansion. Since 1941, when my own board chairman joined the trustees, she has seen UC's budget rise from $3 million to $120 million. Its student body increased in the sixties alone by 75 percent, its faculty by 96 percent, its space by 300 percent.

For administrators, growth became its own object, without form, plan, or coherence. "Management by addition" added programs much as a supermarket stocks its shelves, taking any grab bag that offered funds, without thought for its relevance to teaching and knowledge or for its consequences. Sheer monstrous size became higher education's Achilles' heel. The excess credentialism of employers, abetted by witless counselors and demanding parents, jammed campuses with millions of students who did not really want to be there, who were all dressed up with no place to go, and who often treated college as two more years of high school—with ashtrays. The growing impersonality of multiversities brought first apathy, then anomie, then alienation—flaring into the 1964 Berkeley demonstrations and the Columbia riots and culminating in the 1970 Kent State-Cambodia crisis.

Now the merry-go-round is over, the music has stopped, and the piper must be paid.

Our overgrown universities are confronted with a sharp decline in the number of customers (high school graduates), and the rate of decline will sharpen. The public increasingly demands that higher education earn its future support by proving that its products have some direct relation to the job needs of the society. Where formerly six new faculty members were hired for every one who died or retired, now the ratio is only one to one and may grow less. In the next decade scores of small, private colleges may go under for lack of funds. Others, stifled by a tenure system, watch their faculties grow older and less flexible while angry, frustrated, younger teachers find themselves the captives of dwindling mobility, fewer job offerings, and less chance for advancement on merit.

All our major institutions, particularly but not exclusively the university, are afflicted with a threefold sense of loss: loss of community, loss of purpose, and loss of power.

Perhaps there was never a true "university community" any more than a Camelot. But the image does suggest a time when professors recognized their colleagues on sight and could even remember the name of a senior who asked for a recommendation to a graduate school. Today the faculty, once unified by a common definition of the nature and purposes of scholarship, is fragmented into competing professional citadels. Many have shifted their concern from the intellectual and moral content of education to privilege and ritual.

Students in the multiversity find very little real personal contact or summoning call of the spirit. The real enemy is not anarchy but apathy. Alumni, too, are estranged; many of the older ones are outraged by the weird sea of changes on the campus they remember, while the younger feel no affectionate bond for the institution. And the greatest loss of community, the greatest estrangement, is among the general public—the citizens and parents and their mirror images in legislatures and Congress—on whom the very life of public institutions depends and who are no longer at all sure it is a life worth saving.

With the loss of community has come the loss of power.

For example, at Cincinnati we have not only a faculty senate and a student senate but 69 other committees that are involved, in one way or another, in university governance— including a junior faculty committee, a black faculty committee, and a Jewish faculty council. (In all fairness I must note that despite the difficulties in touching base with all these groups they all have tried to cooperate with, and be supportive of, my administration.) Vast splintering and fragmentation arise from the new populism of those who felt denied in the past and who, rightly, want to be consulted in those decisions that affect them. All this is supposed to add up to "participatory democracy" but adds up, instead, to a cave of the winds where the most that can usually be agreed upon is to do nothing (like the bumper sticker "My Vote Cancels Yours").

As for the purposes of higher education, they became blurred indeed in the quarter-century of postwar expansion. As long as the money poured in and the sky was the limit, there was no visible need to choose between and among programs. One inevitable result was that each university and college began to resemble all the others, becoming a sort of service station from which a student could pluck what he wanted. Now, as the flow of resources and students dries up, colleges and universities are forced for the first time to determine what is essential and what is expendable. A tangle of commitments that were none too purposefully acquired now demands what I call "creative retraction"— a task made all the more difficult and painful by the haphazard, heedless way that Topsy grew.

Unquestionably, universities are among the worst-managed institutions in the country. Hospitals and some state and city administrations may be as bad; no business or industry except Penn Central can possibly be. One reason, incredibly enough, is that universities—which have studied everything from government to Persian mirrors and the number "7"—have never deeply studied their own administration.

The University of Cincinnati, with a staff of 6,000, is the second-largest employer (after General Electric) in Greater Cincinnati. It is in the hotel business (high-rise dorms housing 4,000 students), the restaurant business (ten, all told), and the investment business (a $53-million endowment portfolio), and it must manage a total plant bigger than many utilities.

Its situation is complicated because it is extremely labor-intensive (instructional compensation is 84 percent of the budget) and extremely vulnerable to inflation. And, unlike industry, it has not increased "productivity" (only the construction industry matches education's failure to increase its productivity in 25 years). It is complicated further by being almost uniquely "flat" in its managerial structure. That structure is not "transitive," as it is in business, where executives can expect an orderly rise from step one to step two as their experience and abilities merit. In the university the final locus of power is really the individual professor, who can be "transitive" only to the extent of heading his department; he advances along a *competence* hierarchy, not a *power* hierarchy—one that confers influence and status but not the ability to issue orders or to confer emoluments. In sum, it is society's closest realization of the pure model of anarchy; i.e., the locus of decision making is the individual.

This is the cat's cradle in which university presidents are presently enmeshed. The crisis calls for leadership, but leaders aren't leading. They're consulting, pleading, temporizing, martyrizing, trotting, putting out fires, either avoiding or taking the heat, and spending too much energy in doing both. They've got sweaty palms, and they're scared. One reason is that many of them don't have the faintest concept of what leadership is all about. Like Auden's captain, they are studying navigation while the ship is sinking.

In my moment of truth, that weary 4 A.M. in my trivia-cluttered office, and in the reflective hours of the following summer, I began trying to straighten out in my own mind what the university president should be doing and not doing, what his true priorities should be, how he must lead. I daresay they apply to *all* presidents, *all* leaders, in whatever type of institution.

Lead, not *manage*. There is an important difference. Many an institution is very well managed and very poorly led. It may excel in the ability to handle each day all the routine inputs—yet may never ask whether the routine should be done at all.

Frequently, as I have noted, my best, most enthusiastic deputies unwittingly keep me from working any fundamental change. One, for example, was wheedling me into a personal "liaison" visit to the manager of a huge, new government complex scheduled to be our neighbor. I was about to accept this suggestion, but the lesson from my moment of truth intervened. "Look," I said. "If I go, all I'll hear is things the manager is going to want from the provost, from the librarian, and so on. I'll have to come back and relay these things to them. I may not do so nearly as clearly or persuasively as he would firsthand; furthermore, they might be less cooperative."

All of us find ourselves acting on routine problems because they are the easiest things to handle; we hesitate to get involved too early in the bigger ones—we collude, as it were, in the unconscious conspiracy to immerse us in routine. In the past year I have talked with many new presidents of widely ranging enterprises, and each one has told me the biggest mistake he made was to take on too much, as if proving oneself depended on providing instant solutions and success were dependent on immediate achievements.

My entrapment in routine made me realize another thing: People were following the old army game. They did not want to take the responsibility, or bear the consequences, of decisions they properly should make. The motto was "Let's push up the tough ones." The consequence was that everybody and anybody was dumping his "wet babies" (as the old State Department hands call them) on my desk, when I had neither the diapers nor the information to take care of them.

So I have decided the president's first priority—the sine qua non of effective leadership—is to create around him an "executive constellation" to run the office of the president. It can be a mixed bag—some vice-presidents, some presidential assistants. All of the group must be compatible in the sense that they can work together but neither uniform nor conformist in the sense of yes men—they will be individuals who know *more* than the president does about everything within their areas of competency and can attend to it without dropping their wet babies on his desk. They must be people who take very seriously the functions of the office of the president. They ask what those functions are now and what they should be. They ask what various individuals want to do, are motivated to do, and are competent to do. And they try to work out the "fit."

What should the president himself do? He should be a *conceptualist*. That's something more than being just an

28

"idea man." It means a leader with entrepreneurial vision and the time to spend thinking about the forces that will affect the destiny of his institution. He must educate his board members so that they not only understand the necessity of distinguishing between leadership and management but also can protect the chief executive from getting enmeshed in routine machinery. If he fails to do this, the directors or trustees will collude with the other constituencies to enmesh him—be more concerned about putting out fires than considering whether the building is worth saving.

The leader must create for his institution clear-cut and measurable goals based on advice from all elements of the community. He must be allowed to proceed toward those goals without being crippled by bureaucratic machinery that saps his strength, energy, and initiative. He must be allowed to take risks, to embrace error, to use his creativity to the hilt and encourage faculty and students to use theirs.

Man on a white horse? Some would say so. But consider the situation of the President of the United States, as Richard Neustadt portrays it: "Underneath our images of Presidents-in-boots, astride decisions, are the half-observed realities of Presidents-in-sneakers, stirrups in hand, trying to induce particular department heads, or Congressmen, or Senators, to climb aboard."

I don't want to ride a white horse. I'll settle for a dray horse, even one ready for the glue works. All I want to do is to get one foot in the stirrup.

Assuming I can do so, what goals would I wish to shape? What directions would I offer to help make the university control events rather than, as in the past, being controlled by them? Here are a few, necessarily brief daubs at the future's canvas.

Outside the university, more educational consortia are

needed, perhaps spanning entire regions and embracing public and private institutions alike. In addition, we must establish a direct and seminal relation with the public schools around us, and with the deteriorating neighborhoods where they chiefly cluster.

Within the university, reforms often talked about must, in fact, be carried out. For one thing, faculty tenure must be taken seriously—and by that I mean we must have systematic evaluation of performance, something that has rarely been done in the academic world but has become accepted in business and industry. Tenure was meant not to shield incompetence but rather to give a strong measure of economic security in order to protect academic freedom. For another thing, we will have to increase "efficiency." New techniques are available—from computerized instruction to cable TV. For still another thing, all top administrators, including the president, should be placed on term appointments. Let the leader lead; if he doesn't move the institution measurably toward agreed-upon goals within a certain number of years, oust him.

Above and beyond the set of problems such actions would help to solve lies a larger set. It relates to the nature of work in our society. To begin with, more and more of our well-educated young are eager to enter into some occupation related to the "management of human services." (A majority of students at the top 100 universities, according to a recent Office of Education report, indicate that's what they want to do.) At the same time there is a growing need for these services among the poor, the old, the infirm, and all those people left, not "beyond" the melting pot, but "behind" it. We seem to have no viable mechanism for bringing those individuals with the talent and the drive to help together with those individuals who require such help.

What's needed is some new social invention, equivalent to Henry Ford's assembly line, that will create an appropriate mechanism for this badly needed fusion.

Universities can help. But, as matters stand now, interested students have a fairly difficult time in finding the sorts of curriculums or "majors" that would enable them to learn about the art and science of the development, delivery, and management of human services. At least, they seem to find the university not altogether congenial or forthcoming in this area. Yet, in any case, by 1980 fully 75 percent of the American labor force will be working in "service" activities, many of them carried on by giant public institutions (in education, health, welfare, and so on).

In the light of these facts, what should we be doing?

We should create more cooperative (work-study) educational programs. They should embrace not only departments and colleges that have traditionally used them, such as business, engineering, and architectural design, but those that haven't. I mean, of course, the departments most responsible for general, or liberal, education; usually they are found in the arts and sciences.

We should create co-op programs for faculty, too. Especially in the professional areas, faculty would profit enormously by sustained experience as practitioners in their areas of competence. Indeed, rather than the stale fad of "interdisciplinary" teaching or research, it might be wiser to create opportunities for faculty to engage in "meta-disciplinary" work—that is, work in the occupational sector related or potentially related to their discipline. Professors of education, of business, of sociology, of political science not only would profit personally and professionally from such experiences but would eventually add to the body of knowledge that defines their "fields."

Changes are being made, though not rapidly enough in my view, to create carefully chosen experimental components (not just co-op jobs) that would augment the theoretical/cognitive/abstract side of education. Medical schools manage (sometimes clumsily, but nevertheless they manage) to provide a system that combines classroom work and clinical apprenticeship.

Two-year colleges, despite their popularity and enormous growth over the past decade and a half, must concern themselves with the general traditions of the sciences, humanities, and social sciences. We've produced enough "trained idiots," enough specialists with a "trained incapacity." Segmented education, without the ability to make the right connections among scientific, humanistic, and sociocultural concerns, helps to create segmented and compartmentalized people when we desperately need generalists. We can't afford to educate a "technostructure" without this base in our two-year colleges any more than we can in our four-year colleges. All of this means that our educational "futures," to use the jargon of the day, must once again pay special attention to the arts, to the sciences, to the humanities—in short, to a really vital and integrated liberal education. Against the pressures of a totally utilitarian education, this voice must be not only protected but amplified.

In order to keep our huge university physical plants at full capacity, as well as to add badly needed tuition dollars, industry and government should create mini-sabbaticals for their people. Many employees could profit both themselves and their sponsoring organizations through advanced studies, simple "repotting," or some other form of continuing education.

It isn't only for economic reasons that this "new clientele" should be encouraged. (At the present time it is anything but encouraged; try calling your local college or university to ask how to register as a part-time student in order to take one graduate course during the day.) It's just possible that "older people" (those over 25!) may enrich and animate our campuses in a way that hasn't occurred since the golden days of the GI Bill of Rights. It's just possible that people with work experience, plus commitment to learning, will turn out to be the best students we've ever had. It's just possible that age diversity may be as exciting as ethnic and religious diversity—and perhaps more so (I suspect that there will be far greater integration among the ages than has yet arrived among the races). I've never yet read a novel in which at least three generations didn't play a role; that may soon prove to be true for higher education as well.

In sum, I believe that changes in higher education during the seventies will come about not merely for the sake of change but, rather, for the sake of humanity and the future of our human organizations. Without, however, a thorough understanding of the processes of change, our leadership needs, and the social architecture of our giant, multifaceted institutions, we all might just as well continue to work diligently on blue-ribbon "task force" committees. Nothing insures the status quo so much as putting the best minds and best talents on these task forces. For their reports continue to get better as our problems get worse.

THE OPTIONS

In speaking out one loses influence.
The chance for change by pleas and prayer is gone.
The chance to modify the devil's deeds
As critic from within is still my hope.
To quit the club! Be outside looking in!
This outsideness, this unfamiliar land,
From which few travelers ever get back in . . .
I fear to break; I'll work within for change.

Barbara Garson, *MacBird!*

RESIGNATION
FOR PRINCIPLE

No MATTER how often Daniel Ellsberg reminded the public that not he but a seemingly endless war in Indochina was at issue, I always found that it was Ellsberg the man who touched the imagination. One couldn't help speculating on his personal odyssey from loyal insider to defiant outsider, from organization man to prison-risking dissident.

It is the process of that change of heart that fascinates me. What interaction of man and organization produces a commitment like the younger Ellsberg's and then leads only a few years later to equally passionate rejection? How much, I wonder, of the Ellsberg affair is idiosyncratic and how much reflects general principles of organizational life? After all, Ellsberg was not the first government adviser to become suspicious of the work in which he had engaged.

What was singular about Ellsberg is that he found a dramatic way to make his dissent articulate. The organizational ethic is typically so strong that even the individual who dissents and opts for the outside by resigning or otherwise dissociating himself does so with organization-serving

This chapter is reprinted from an article prepared in collaboration with Patricia Ward Biederman.

37

discretion. Ellsberg may not have broken the law, but he surely did something more daring. He broke the code. He not only spoke out, he produced documentation of his disillusionment.

The stakes are rarely as great, but many people who work in large, bureaucratic organizations find themselves in a position similar to Ellsberg's. They oppose some policy, and they quickly learn that bureaucracies do not tolerate dissent. What then? They have several options: They can capitulate. Or they can remain within the group and try to win the majority over to their own position, enduring the frustration and ambiguity that go with this option. Or they can resign. Remaining can be an excruciating experience of public loyalty and private doubt. But what of resigning? Superficially resignation seems an easy out, but it also has its dark and conflictful side. And, if resignation is the choice, the problem of how to leave, silently or openly voicing one's position, still remains.

These options are a universal feature of organizational life and yet virtually nothing has been written on the dynamics of dissent in organizations, although a recent book by Harvard political economist Albert O. Hirschman almost single-handedly makes up for past deficiencies.* Oddly enough, the book still remains "underground," largely unread by the wide audience touched by the processes Hirschman describes.

I first began seriously considering the question of resignation and other expressions of dissent as organizational phenomena in the spring of 1970. At that time I had just resigned as acting executive vice-president of the State University of New York at Buffalo. As so often happens, my

* *Exit, Voice, and Loyalty.* Harvard University Press, 1970.

interest in the phenomenon grew out of unpleasant personal experience. I had resigned in protest against what I considered undue use of force on the part of the university's acting president in dealing with a series of student strikes on our campus that spring.

In my case, resigning turned out to be a remarkably ineffective form of protest for many reasons, notably my decision to retain another administrative position while resigning the acting post. The distinction between the positions was clear only to other members of the administration, and the public generally interpreted my equivocal exit as a halfhearted protest.

When I tried to analyze why it was ineffective, I found that my experience was hardly unique, that most large organizations, including government agencies and universities, have well-oiled adaptive mechanisms for neutralizing dissent. The individual who can force the organization into a public confrontation, as Ellsberg did, is rare indeed.

The garden-variety resignation is an innocuous act, no matter how righteously indignant the individual who tenders it. The act is made innocuous by a set of organization-serving conventions that few resignees are able (or even willing, for a variety of personal reasons) to break. When the properly socialized dissenter resigns, he tiptoes out. A news release is sent to the media on the letterhead of the departing one's superior. "I today accepted with regret the resignation of Mister/Doctor Y," it reads. The *pro forma* statement rings pure tin in the discerning ear, but this is the accepted ritual nonetheless. One retreats under a canopy of smiles, with verbal bouquets and exchanges, however insincere, of mutual respect. The last official duty of the departing one is to keep his mouth shut. The rules of play require that the last word goes to those who remain inside.

The purpose served by this convention is a purely institutional one. Announcement of a resignation is usually a sign of disharmony and possibly real trouble within an organization. But, without candid follow-up by the individual making the sign, it is an empty gesture. The organization reasons, usually correctly, that the muffled troublemaker will soon be forgotten. With the irritant gone, the organization pursues its chosen course, subject only to the casual and untrained scrutiny of the general public.

The striving of organizations for harmony is less a conscious program than a consequence of the structure of large organizations. Cohesiveness in such organizations results from a commonly held set of values, beliefs, norms, and attitudes. In other words, an organization is also an appreciative system in which those who do not share the common set, the common point of view, are by definition deviant, marginal, outsiders.

Ironically, this pervasive emphasis on harmony does not serve organizations particularly well. Unanimity leads rather quickly to stagnation, which, in turn, invites change by nonevolutionary means. The fact that the organizational deviant, the individual who "sees" things differently, may be the institution's vital and only link with, for lack of a better term, some new, more apt paradigm does not make the organization value him any more. Most organizations would rather risk obsolescence than make room for the nonconformists in their midst.

This is most true when such intolerance is most suicidal; that is, when the issues involved are of major importance (or when important people have taken a very strong or a personal position). On matters such as whether to name a new product "Corvair" or "Edsel," or whether to establish a franchise in Peoria or Oshkosh, dissent is reasonably well tolerated, even welcomed, as a way of insuring that the best of all possible alternatives is finally implemented. But when it comes to war or peace, life or death, growth or organizational stagnation, fighting or withdrawing, reform or status quo—desperately important matters—dissent is typically seen as fearful. Exactly at that point in time when it is most necessary to consider the possible consequences of a wide range of alternatives, a public show of consensus becomes an absolute value to be defended no matter what the human cost.

Unanimity, or at least its public show, is so valued within the organizational context that it often carries more weight with an individual than his own conscience. Thus we noted in the March 31, 1971, issue of *The New York Times* that "Muskie regrets silence on war" and wishes that he had made public as far back as 1965 his "real doubts about involvement in the Vietnam war." Instead, he said, "he voiced his concerns privately to President Johnson." "There are two ways," he said, "and they're both legitimate ways of trying to influence public policy. And I can guess the tendency is, when the President is a member of your own party and you're a senator, to try to express your doubts directly to him, in order to give him a chance to get the benefit of your views." Senator Muskie said he often had done that, "but wished that I'd expressed my doubts publicly at that time." The article goes on to say that Muskie "was far less hesitant to criticize President Nixon's conduct of the war."

In an adjoining article about Humphrey, the *Times* reported him as describing to a student audience publicly for the first time the pressure he had been under from President Johnson not to speak out on the Vietnam issue.

Many times during the first month of the 1968 campaign, he recalled, he had wanted to speak out more forcefully on the Vietnam issue only to be dissuaded by the President. This, he said, posed a personal dilemma. On the one side, he said, he saw his chances for winning the Presidency slipping away. But if he sought headlines on the Vietnam issue by taking a more critical stance, he said, he was being warned by the President that he would jeopardize the delicate negotiations then under way to bring South Vietnam and the Vietcong to the Paris negotiating table.

"That's the God's truth. . . . How would you like to be in that jam?" Humphrey asked a student.

Actually, Humphrey's "jam" is a classic one. A member in good standing of an organization, in this case the Johnson Administration, suddenly finds himself opposed to his superior and his colleagues in regard to some policy. If the policy is relatively unimportant or not yet firm, the objection may be absorbed by bargaining or compromise. If the issue at stake is actually trivial, it may simply be avoided. But, if the issue is important and the dissenter adamant, the gulf begins to widen.

At first, the dissenter tries to exert all possible influence over the others, tries to bring the others around. In Albert Hirschman's compact terminology, this is the option of *voice*. Short of calling a press conference, this option can be exercised in several ways from simply grumbling to threatening to resign. But usually the individual gives voice to his dissatisfaction in a series of private confrontations like those of Muskie and Humphrey with Johnson. When these fail, as they usually do, he must face the possibility of resigning (or, as Hirschman calls it, exercising the option to *exit*).

Resigning becomes a reasonable alternative as soon as

voice begins to fail. The individual realizes that hours of sincere, patient argument have come to nothing. He realizes that his influence within the organization is waning, and so, probably, is his loyalty. If he stays on, he risks becoming an organizational eunuch, an individual of no influence publicly supporting a policy against his will, his judgment, his personal value system, at times even his professional code.

As bleak as this prospect is, exit on matters of principle is still a distinctly uncommon response to basic institutional conflict. This is particularly true of American politics. In many nations with parliamentary systems, principled resignation from high office is common. But in the United States the concept of exit as a political act has never taken hold. The Walter Hickels are the exception. The last time a cabinet official left in protest and said why was when Labor Secretary Martin Durkin resigned because President Eisenhower refused to support his proposed amendments to the Taft-Hartley Act.*

In a postmortem on the Johnson Administration, James Reston stated that the record clearly shows that the art of resigning on principle from high government positions in the United States has almost disappeared. Anthony Eden and Duff Cooper left Neville Chamberlain's cabinet with a clear, detailed explanation of why they could no longer be identified with the policy of appeasement. Nobody does that now. Most of those who remained at the critical period of escalation of the war in Vietnam gave the President the

---

* This article was, of course, written well before the famous Saturday Night Massacre when both Attorney General Elliott Richardson and his immediate successor resigned and very publicly refused to obey President Nixon's order to fire Special Prosecutor Archibald Cox. In another clear case of public protest, President Ford's press secretary, J. F. ter-Horst, resigned after Ford pardoned Nixon.

loyalty they owed to the country. Now, in private life, some of them are wondering whether this was really in the national interest.

What accounts for our national reluctance to resign and our willingness, when forced to take the step, to settle for a "soft exit," without clamor, without a public statement of principle, and ideally without publicity? Tremendous institutional pressures and personal rationalizations work together to dissuade the dissident from exit in favor of voice. Most of us would much rather convince the boss or top group to see "reason" rather than quit. Resignation is defiant, an uncomfortable posture for most organization men (including politicians and academics). Worse, it smacks of failure, the worst of social diseases among the achievement-oriented. So, instead of resigning, we reason to ourselves that the organization could go from bad to worse if we resigned. This may be the most seductive rationalization of all. Meanwhile, we have become more deeply implicated in the policy that we silently oppose, making extrication progressively more difficult.

If resignation cannot be avoided, there are selfish reasons for doing it quietly. Most resignees would like to work again. Only Nader's Raiders love a blabbermouth. Speaking out is not likely to enhance one's marketability. A negative aura haunts the visibly angry resignee, while the individual who leaves a position ostensibly to return to business, family, teaching, or research reenters the job market without any such cloud. Many resignees prefer a low profile simply because they are aware that issues change. Why undermine one's future effectiveness by making a noisy but ineffectual stand?

However selfish the reasons, the organization reaps the major benefits when an individual chooses to resign quietly.

A decorous exit conceals the underlying dissension that prompted the resignation in the first place. And the issue at contest is almost sure to be obscured by the speech making.

Like the Zen tea ceremony, resigning is a ritual, and woe to the man who fails to do it according to the rules. For example, when Fred Friendly resigned as president of CBS News in 1966 over the airing of Vietnam hearings, he sinned by releasing a news story *before* the chairman of the board, William S. Paley, could distribute his own release. Friendly writes in his memoir of this episode:

Around two o'clock a colleague suggested that I should have called Paley, who was in Nassau, and personally read my letter [of resignation] to him over the phone. When I called Stanton to ask him if he had read my letter to the chairman, he said that he had just done so, and that Paley wanted me to call him. When I did, Paley wanted to know only if I had released my letter; when I told him that I had, all useful communication ceased. "You volunteered to me last week that you would not make a public announcement," he said. . . . The last thing the chairman said to me was: "Well, if you hadn't put out that letter, maybe we could still have done something." I answered that my letter was "after the fact, long after."

Paley's response is explicable only if we remember that the *fact* of resignation and the *reasons* behind it are subordinated in the organizational scheme to the issue of institutional face saving. A frank resignation is regarded by the organization as an act of betrayal. (To some degree, this is, of course, an issue of personal face saving. Those in power may wish for institutional harmony in part as a protection against personal criticism.)

Because a discreet resignation amounts to no protest at all, a soft exit lifts the opprobrium of organizational deviation from the resignee. When Dean Acheson bowed out as Under Secretary of the Treasury in 1933 after a dispute with F.D.R. over fiscal policy, his discretion was boundless and F.D.R. was duly appreciative. Some years later, when another official left with less politesse, sending the White House a sharp criticism of the President's policies, Roosevelt returned the letter with the tart suggestion that the man ought to "ask Dean Acheson how a gentleman resigns."

But, "hard" or "soft," exit remains the option of last resort in organizational life. Remarkably, the individual who is deeply opposed to some policy often opts for public acquiescence and private frustration. He may continue to voice his opposition to his colleagues, but they are able to neutralize his protest in various ways. Thus we see George Ball becoming the official devil's advocate of the Johnson Administration. As George E. Reedy writes:

During President Johnson's Administration I watched George Ball play the role of devil's advocate with respect to foreign policy. The cabinet would meet and there would be an overwhelming report from Robert McNamara, another overwhelming report from Dean Rusk, another overwhelming report from McGeorge Bundy. Then five minutes would be set aside for George Ball to deliver his dissent, and because they expected him to dissent, they automatically discounted whatever he said. This strengthened them in their own convictions because the cabinet members could quite honestly say: "We heard both sides of this issue discussed." Well, they heard it with wax in their ears. I think that the moment you appoint an official devil's advocate you solidify the position he is arguing against.*

One can hardly imagine a predicament more excruciating than Ball's. Often an individual in such conflict with the

* *Twilight of the Presidency.* Norton, 1975.

46

rest of his organization simply removes himself, if not physically then by shifting his concern from the issues to practical problems of management and implementation. He distracts himself. Townsend Hoopes suggests that this was the case with Robert McNamara. According to Hoopes, who was Under Secretary of the Air Force, there was growing evidence in the autumn of 1967 that the President and McNamara were growing further and further apart in their attitudes toward escalating the Vietnam war. Hoopes saw in McNamara the fatigue and loneliness of a man "in deep doubt" as to the course the war was taking. But, writes Hoopes:

Owing to his own strict conception of loyalty to the President, McNamara found it officially necessary to deny all doubt and, by his silence, to discourage doubt in his professional associates and subordinates. . . . The result of McNamara's ambivalence, however, was to create a situation of dreamlike unreality for those around him. *His staff meetings during this period were entirely barren affairs: a technical briefing, for example, on the growing strength of air defenses around Hanoi, but no debate on what this implied for the U.S. bombing effort, and never the slightest disclosure of what the President or the Secretary of State might consider the broad domestic and international implications to be.* It was an atmosphere that worked to neutralize those who were the natural supporters of his concerns about the war.* [Italics are for emphasis.]

What Hoopes describes is ethical short-circuiting. Conflict-torn McNamara busies himself with the minutiae of war planning because lists of numbers and cost estimates have a distracting if illusory moral neutrality. According to Hoopes, toward the end of McNamara's tenure the despair-

* *The Limits of Intervention.* McKay, 1970.

ing secretary stopped questioning the military and political significance of sending 206,000 more troops into Indochina and concentrated in the short time he had on the logistical problems of getting them to the port of debarkation safely and efficiently.

One sees a remarkably similar displacement of energy from moral or political concerns to managerial or technological ones in the career of Albert Speer. (I do not mean to label McNamara a Fascist by literary association.) The pages of *Inside the Third Reich* reveal that Speer dealt with ambivalence brought on by intense organizational stress in a remarkably similar way. Speer did not allow his growing personal reservations about Hitler to interfere with his meticulous carrying out of administrative duties. Speer kept the Nazi war machine running in high gear and increasingly productive until 1945. As Eugene Davidson writes: "A man like Speer, working with blueprints, ordering vast projects, is likely to exhaust himself in manipulation, in transforming the outer world, in carrying out production goals with all the means at hand."

Whether such activity exhausts an individual to the point of moral numbness is questionable, but certainly the nature of the large organization makes it possible for a McNamara or an Albert Speer or an Ellsberg (while at Rand), for that matter, to work toward an ultimately immoral end without an immediate sense of personal responsibility or guilt. Organizations are by definition systems of increased differentiation and specialization, and thus the morality of the organization is the morality of segmented acts. As Charles Reich wrote in *The New Yorker*,*

* The material was subsequently published as part of a full-length book, *The Greening of America*, Random House, 1970.

A scientist who is doing his specialized duty to further research and knowledge develops a substance called napalm. Another specialist makes policy in the field of our nation's foreign affairs. A third is concerned with the most modern weaponry. A fourth manufactures what the defense authorities require. A fifth drops napalm from an airplane where he is told to do so.

In this segmented environment, any one individual can easily develop tunnel vision, concentrating on the task at hand, completing his task with a sense of accomplishment, however sinister the collective result of all these individual jobs well done. This segmented structure characteristic of all large organizations encourages indifference and evasion of responsibility. A benefit of membership in such an organization is insurance against the smell of burning flesh. Speer, for example, still does not seem particularly troubled by the horrors of slave labor in his wartime munitions plants even when making his unique public confession.

Speer reports that it never occurred to him to resign even though he was aware of what his loss would do to hasten the end of Hitler's regime. Faced with a much more subtle and complex situation, McNamara seriously considered resigning, according to Hoopes. But that he did not do so in 1967 when his doubts were so oppressive is remarkable. Hoopes provides a fascinating clue to McNamara's reluctance to resign or even to voice his uneasiness in any except the most private audiences with the President. In the following short portrait by Hoopes in his book *The Limits of Intervention*, we see McNamara wrestling with an ingrained organizational ethic stronger than his own intelligence and instinct:

Accurately regarded by the press as the one moderate member of the inner circle, he continued to give full public support to the Administration's policy, including specific endorsement of successive manpower infusions and progressively wider and heavier bombing efforts. Inside the Pentagon he seemed to discourage dissent among his staff associates by the simple tactic of being unreceptive to it; he observed, moreover, so strict a sense of privacy in his relationship with the President that he found it virtually impossible to report even to key subordinates what he was telling the President or what the President was saying and thinking. . . .

All of this seemed to reflect a well-developed philosophy of executive management relationships, derived from his years in industry; its essence was the belief that a busy, overworked chairman of the board should be spared the burden of public differences among his senior vice-presidents. Within such a framework, he could argue the case for moderation with the President—privately, selectively, and intermittently. But the unspoken corollary seemed to be that, whether or not his counsel of moderation were followed, there could arise no issue or difference with President Johnson sufficient to require his resignation—whether to enlighten public opinion or avoid personal stultification. It was this corollary that seemed of doubtful applicability to the problems and obligations of public office. *McNamara gave evidence that he had ruled out resignation because he believed that the situation would grow worse if he left the field to Rusk, Rostow, and the Joint Chiefs. But also because the idea ran so strongly against the grain of his temperament and his considered philosophy of organizational effectiveness.*

Does this mean that McNamara would not resign because quitting violated some personal notion of honor? Or does it mean that he believed that dissent and "organizational effectiveness" are negatively correlated? I suspect that the latter is closer to the truth. Like any other corporation president, McNamara was raised on organizational folklore. One of the central myths is that the show of unanimity is always desirable. That this belief is false and even dangerous does not limit its currency.

Yes, there are times when discretion is required. Clearly organizations should not fight constantly in public. But what is the gain of forbidding at all costs and at all times any emotional give-and-take between colleagues? A man has an honest difference of opinion with the organizational powers. Why must he be silenced or domesticated or driven out so that the public can continue to believe—falsely—that organizational life is without strife? And yet organizations continue to assume the most contrived postures in order to maintain the illusion of harmony—postures like lying to the public.

Our inability to transcend the dangerous notion that we don't wash our dirty linen in public verges on the schizophrenic. It implies not only that dissent is bad but that our public institutions, such as governments, are made up not of men but saints who never engage in such vulgar and offensive activities. Thus government strives to be regarded as a hallowed shrine where, as George Reedy reports from his experience as White House press secretary under President Johnson, "the meanest lust for power can be sanctified and the dullest wit greeted with reverential awe."

In fact, organizations, including governments, are vulgar, sweaty, plebeian; if they are to be viable, they must create an institutional environment where a fool can be called a fool and all actions and motivations are duly and closely scrutinized for the inevitable human flaws and failures. In a democracy, meanness, dullness, and corruption are always amply represented. They are not entitled to protection from the same rude challenges that such qualities must face in the "real" world. When banal politeness is assigned a higher value than accountability or truthfulness, the result is an Orwellian world where the symbols of speech are manipulated to create false realities.

"Loyalty" is often given as a reason or pretext for muffling dissent. A variation on this is the claim that candor "gives comfort to the enemy." Ellsberg's national loyalty was repeatedly questioned in connection with his release of the so-called Pentagon Papers. In the first three installments of the document as run in the *Times*, practically nothing that wasn't well known was revealed. A few details, an interesting admission or two, but basically nothing that had not come to light earlier in other less controversial articles and books on the Indochina war. But government officials trying to suppress the publication of the classified material chose to make much of the "foreign consequences" of its release. "You may rest assured," a government official was quoted as saying by the Buffalo *Evening News*, "that no one is reading this series any more closely than the Soviet Embassy."

All the foregoing pressures against registering dissent can be subsumed under the clumsy label of "loyalty." In fact, they represent much more subtle personal and organizational factors, including deep-rooted psychological dependence, authority problems, simple ambition, co-optive mechanisms (the "devil's advocacy" technique), pressure to be a member of the club and fear of being outside looking in, adherence to the myth that gentlemen settle their differences amicably and privately, fear of disloyalty in the form of giving comfort to "the enemy," and, very often, that powerful Prospero aspiration: the conviction that one's own "reasonable" efforts will keep things from going from bad to worse.

There is a further broad cultural factor that must be considered before the other defenses against exit can be understood. It simply doesn't make sense for a man as intelligent and analytically sophisticated as Robert McNamara to delude himself that he couldn't quit because "duty called." Duty to whom? Not to his own principles. Nor, as he saw it, to the nation's welfare. McNamara's real loyalty was to the code of the "organizational society" in which most of us live out our entire active careers.

Ninety percent of the employed population of this country works in formal organizations. Status, position, a sense of competence and accomplishment are all achieved in our culture through belonging to these institutions. What you *do* determines, to a large extent, what you *are*. "My son, the doctor" is not only the punch line of a thousand Jewish jokes. It is a neat formulation of a significant fact about our culture. Identification with a profession or other organization is a real-life passport to identity, to selfhood, to self-esteem. You are what you do, and work in our society (as in all other industrialized societies) is done in large, complex, bureaucratic structures. If one leaves the organization, particularly with protest, one is nowhere, like a character in a Beckett play—without role, without the props of office, without ambience or setting.

In fact, a few more resignations would be good for individual consciences and good for the country. Looking back, veteran diplomat Robert Murphy could recall only one occasion when he thought he should have resigned. The single instance was the Berlin Blockade of 1948–1949, which he thought the United States should have challenged more vigorously. "My resignation almost certainly would not have affected events," he wrote in regret, "but if I had resigned, I would feel better today about my own part in that episode." *Time* magazine, from which Murphy's quotation was taken, goes on to say in its essay:

In the long run, the country would probably feel better, too, if a few more people were ready to quit for their convictions. It might be a little unsettling. But it could have a tonic effect on American politics, for it would give people the assurance that men who stay truly believe in what they are doing.

My own resignation was a turning point. The decision represented the first time in many years of organizational life that I had been able to say, "No, I cannot allow myself to be identified with that particular policy," the first time I had risked being an outsider rather than trying to work patiently within the system for change. Many factors entered into the decision, but in the last analysis my reason for resigning was an intensely personal one. I did not want to say, a month or two months after the police came onto campus, "Well, I was against that move at the time." I think it is important for everyone in a decision-making position in any of our institutions to speak out. And if we find it impossible to continue on as administrators because we are at total and continuous odds with institutional policy, then I think we must quit and go out shouting. The alternative is petit Eichmannism, and that is too high a price.

SURVIVING
THE REVOLUTION
OF CONSCIOUSNESS

IN THE EARLY 1960s, many of us who made a business out of predicting the future were guilty of a common error. We assumed that certain basic trends of the 1950s—toward bigness, toward interdependence of institutions, toward concentration—would continue unchallenged.

We hoped that the problems caused by technology would be cured by a higher order of technology. That the problems caused by big science would be cured by the breakthroughs of bigger science.

My own book, *The Temporary Society*,* joined in this cult of inevitability; but it tried to suggest ways to infuse these large-scale systems with a more humanistic and democratic bent. I suggested some directions in which we might move to make the people enmeshed in our vast modern hierarchies more aware of each other's human needs. I thought that all the trends of a massive, postindustrial society would continue but that there were ways to make it better, a bit more human. My optimism was based on the expectation of a slow process of incremental reform.

* Written with Philip E. Slater.

What the book missed—what most futurists were incapable of predicting—was that the challenge of the 1960s would not turn out to be liberal and reformist. It would be revolutionary—and from several directions at once.

The vehemence of the black rebellion should have been more predictable, but the social movement which took all of us by surprise was the revolt of white, affluent, educated youth. The revolution in Scarsdale. This is the revolution which tore our universities apart and which is having a profound effect on the business and governmental community. It has forced us to revise most of our ideas about the future.

There are now 7.5 million young people in college. They form a truly vast, new intelligentsia. This intelligentsia hasn't changed that much in quality from the old. After all, the intelligentsia has traditionally remained a bit outside society and lobbed social criticism at the establishment. But it was always a tiny fraction of the population. Suddenly, in America, the intelligentsia has become a major segment of the population. Its representatives are now spreading from the campus into government, business, and the professions —but are continuing to define themselves as critics, as devil's advocates, and as radical reformers.

When this critical intelligentsia formed a tiny percentage of the population, it was perfectly proper to think that those who went to work for TRW and GE would be absorbed into the organization. But today there are simply too many. They are aware of themselves as a community. They are able to support each other's rebellion in ways which were never possible before.

So I believe they will have a profound impact on the world of business—an impact none of us futurists was able to predict but which we must begin to measure now. What will that impact be? What are the demands of their revolution? Unlike the situation in the 1930s, the demands of to-day have very little to do with wages and touch only pe-ripherally on the conditions of work. These revolutionaries are children of the middle class, and they have reached a higher level in the hierarchy of needs. The typical college rebels are the offspring of technocrats, lawyers, and doc-tors. They are interested in creating work situations which bring joy, spontaneity, self-expression, and self-actualiza-tion.

Their new morality is person-centered. It values tech-nology only if the technology serves personal growth and social goals. To the extent that institutions and their leaders fail in fulfilling these goals, they will fail to attract the brightest young people to work in them.

These values and these concerns are producing a second society within the first. This second culture is, in many ways, far clumsier than the massive postindustrial society which provided a model for the futurists. It is a society far less concerned with profit or production. It is—by its own ideology—awkward and participative. The new culture is willing to tolerate inefficiency for the sake of personal de-velopment. A group of kids may take eight months to put up a geodesic dome when they could have a contractor put it up in two days—but they'll do it the slow way. Similarly, they will trade off part of the GNP for a smaller political and economic involvement overseas.

The new culture treasures smallness, human scale, and cultural pluralism. In the past few years, it has produced a host of little communities with those goals. These include all the counterinstitutions of the Left: the free schools, the underground newspapers, the communes. It is an odd parallel to the process by which tiny companies on Route 128 are spun off from the big corporations and universities.

And I think the two derive from many of the same needs—for individuation, for creativity, for more continual human contact with co-workers.

I think leaders today must reckon with the fact that these minisocieties will become increasingly dominant on the American scene. Indeed, they will comprise a whole countertrend which we failed to foresee in the early 1960s, a drive toward smallness, personal diversity, and cultural pluralism.

The next ten years or so will see a very dynamic, sometimes abrasive interaction between the two cultures, old and new. Sometimes the issues will center on social responsibility; sometimes they will deal with suitable ways to combine bigness and smallness, productive efficiency and human scale. I personally think that there are ways to combine these two trends to gain the advantages of both. Of bigness and smallness, of centralized power and cultural diversity.

So far, the "alternative institutions" of the Left—the communes and underground culture—have been the only ways to meet the needs of the young. The big firms have had difficulty attracting talented graduates from the campus, but I still believe that business remains one of the most creative places for designing the jobs which will finally satisfy our young people.

To a large degree, these young people are stuck with us. Despite the fact that their parents are (or have been till recently) affluent, they're going to have to make a living. So they don't have that many options. They can't all make movies or drive cabs or write for underground newspapers, and there are only so many slots in the Peace Corps and VISTA. Many stay on in school for lack of anything more appealing. They seem to be marking time until more attractive institutions can be designed. They're all dressed up with no place to go. At present, none of our institutions offers them much they really like.

Many of our disaffected youth hope that their counter-culture will completely supplant the old corporations and governmental institutions. This seems to me unlikely—but, provided their present disaffection from the private sector can be softened a bit, it seems to me that business has much to offer them. Before it can, however, both sides will have to learn a great deal. And one of the things business and business leaders will have to learn is that social change is here. The revolutions are actually happening. The kids can't be conned.

One of the major problems in working toward this synthesis is that the big firms remain largely unaware of how important, how dynamic these revolutionary forces really are. The corporation is a closed world; and it becomes increasingly difficult, the longer you are inside, to be aware of what is happening just outside the door. It's very hard for a corporation to remain sensitive to social change, but it is vital. You never escape a revolution completely. The longer you wait, the more expensive it is when you find out about it.

Just a few years ago, I was called in as a consultant to the managers of a Chicago department store who paid a very high price to learn what was going on all round them. Their store was partly burned down—a $20-million fire. They had to conclude that it was arson—almost certainly committed by someone black, possibly employed by them. They had one of the most liberal policies with respect to hiring minority groups, but only a tiny fraction of the blacks they'd hired had risen above the clerk or salesperson level.

Right after the fire, the executives brought in some of

the most militant members of the black action groups in Chicago to ask them what had gone wrong. I was there, and it was a stormy session. The meeting was a real shocker for the executives, because they hadn't realized how tough the black revolt had become. And the executives of that store weren't naive men. They weren't conservatives, either.

I'm not sure that management learned anything new, but what these people already knew took on sudden force. It became persuasive after the fire, whereas it hadn't been before. The executives told the militants how proud they were to have blacks working in the store, but the blacks pointed out that there wasn't one black buyer. There weren't any blacks in management. The executives certainly knew that; but, inside a closed world like a corporation, you come to exercise a kind of selective ignorance.

During those bitter days after the fire, these department store executives realized an important point. The entire marketing pattern in the city of Chicago had changed without their really being aware of it—a dreadful blow to the pride of any marketing organization. They had an entirely new clientele—black people. Black people with very different desires, needs, and financial problems. The store hadn't really come to terms with this shifting market.

In addition to being the right and moral thing to do, it made economic sense to have blacks in management. And that's the first step the store took—but it took a $20-million fire before management acted.

By now, most corporations are aware that there is a black revolution going on, though not many have quite figured out what to do about it. But how many firms are really sensitive to the multiple revolutions occurring in our society?

Take women's rights. Very few managers realize that

when women's liberation takes hold—and it's moving extremely fast now—it will make the black revolt seem like a spring zephyr. It's always more painful to have a civil war when you're already integrated.

Few businessmen pay men and women equally, respect women's judgment, and promote them on the same basis as men. Very few institutions have done anything at all about setting up day-care centers so that women can really pursue their careers; this will be one of the biggest issues of the next few years.

For my own part, I welcome it—though nervously, of course. I think women will make excellent managers. Because of their cultural training, I think they're far more capable of absorbing and dealing with conflict than men. Women are also less subject to distortions of power than men. Men are educated to a style of personal ambition which makes their heads swim in situations of power and status.

David Riesman, the Harvard sociologist, once suggested to me that one way to insure the social orientation of science and technology would be to get more women into the field. There is nothing, he said, which would humanize science as much as more women engineers and physicists.

It's very difficult for a corporation to remain sensitive to social change, but it has become increasingly vital. And there are definitely ways for a corporation to learn about social change without a $20-million fire—although they require genuine effort.

In every organization, there are people who are out at the cuticle. In the regular course of work, they make contact with people on the outside and are often the first to sense change. They are salespeople, personnel recruiters, sometimes lawyers. Properly encouraged, they can act as scanners for the company, letting the household executives know what is happening on the outside. Unhappily, they are most often in the impotent departments of the company. They're always muttering about how to change the organization, but they somehow don't affect the fabric of the system.

I think it's terribly important for institutions to recognize and reward these individuals who are at the boundaries of the company. They are interstitial men and women—they connect several worlds and can provide excellent information about the social climate.

One example of an interstitial man is Rowan Wakefield. I knew him as an assistant to the chancellor of the sprawling State University of New York. He had an office in Washington, and his job was to hook people between the two worlds. He helped professors find their way through the Washington research-fund labyrinth. He was virtually autonomous there and very good at spotting opportunities. He was very much attuned to changes in the Washington scene. In essence, he served the function of bringing together two very different social systems. Every company has people who function that way in a less formal capacity.

Thomas Allen writes about how scientific information really gets into a company. He says it rarely comes through journals or consultants. Usually there are one or two people working in the company who keep up a wide range of contacts in the scientific community or make a point of keeping up with the journals. Allen calls these men "gatekeepers"; he says that most of the scientific information which finds its way in comes through them.

He was talking only about the information most directly relevant to the process of scientific innovation. However, almost all information of any kind enters a company that way. There are many kinds of gatekeepers in a company, and they have access to various kinds of worlds. Part of the manager's job is to decide which of these gatekeepers he wants to encourage.

If he believes it is important to be aware of social changes outside the company, he can find ways to encourage access to that information through the black gatekeepers or the radicals on his staff. He might invite them to bring in literature or friends to lecture. That is fairly standard practice in most think tanks, which make it their business to keep in very close touch with the social environment. It may be that keeping up has become an important function in all companies.

The manager might simply tell his social gatekeepers, "Perhaps you can act as our access point to people on the outside. Go ahead. Take some time, bring in people who will challenge us fundamentally in various ways and do it right here in the company. That way we can learn with the least pain about changes which will certainly affect us in any event."

Many times these gatekeepers may not seem like the best company men. They have external constituencies; they have outside interests; they may even have a low commitment to the primary tasks of the organization. But somehow we must develop a reward structure that will encourage people in just that gatekeeping role, because it is absolutely vital to the evolution of organizational goals.

The gatekeepers are the people a consultant looks for when he comes into an organization. I call them variance sensors. They sense discrepancies between what the organization ought to be doing and what it actually is doing. As a result, they're under continual tension. They're good problem identifiers. This makes them, in fact, very useful company men, although they may often seem abrasive to others in the company.

If you're concerned about generating an awareness of the outside environment, then your first job as manager is to recognize these gatekeepers for what they are. To judge whether their "second worlds" are relevant to your organization. And to find ways to help them bring that world into the company where people can learn from it.

Once we've achieved a degree of openness between the rebels and the private sector, once leaders and managers have shown they can be genuinely sensitive to social change, I believe a real process of social experimentation can begin.

Much of the experimentation will deal with ways to combine centralized services with cultural diversity. All our institutions will begin responding to the revolution we're going through now. They'll have to. It's a revolution in consciousness—for the first time in ages we're taking seriously the subjective experiences of people. The changes will be as vast as those which followed our unlocking of the secrets of the atom. I believe the T-group movement and the hippie movement are manifestations of a new consciousness which is giving credibility and validation to a man's or woman's subjective experience: the way each sees the world, his or her own desires.

I think this concern with the subjective will give first priority to finding out how an individual can maintain his integrity in a shifting, turbulent society. Much more attention will have to be paid in colleges and universities to the art and science—the total business—of becoming fully human.

What the kids want to do is understand their identities. Free their personalities. Become human. Learn about what directly concerns them—which at present is politics, rock music, movies, drugs, and religion. Some smart industrialist is going to come along and begin setting up degree-granting Woodstock festivals. Not for year-long bashes—but on a drop-in, drop-out basis.

The universities will probably put a great deal of emphasis on how to create human environments—in both physical and spiritual terms. I can imagine new varieties of Route 128 spinning off these institutions of learning. Little companies would specialize in marketing various social environments. To educate children better, to coordinate health facilities, to sensitize executives. Here is a wealth of exciting careers for the rebels of today.

At present we can see needs, but the markets are still undefined. For example, in New York City there is a tremendous need for computer-aided instruction. But developing and purchasing the technology for that instruction is so expensive that New York can't afford to buy it from the present manufacturers. There's a need and a supplier, but no market.

The real challenge for the young in technology and private enterprise is to see how these needs can be converted into markets. Again, this involves very creative thinking about how to combine the advantages of bigness and smallness.

The revolution in consciousness, however, does not mean that every subjective urge should be accepted. It just means that there must be an increasing sensitivity to the real desires of people.

I was talking the other day to the director of an R&D lab which works on social applications for technology. He emphasized how difficult it is to work with young people these days. They really want to do their own thing, yet his job is somehow to bring a concerted effort out of all these individuals. Some of the young men told him that they had their own projects they wanted to develop in the lab—they weren't really interested in his. Some of the projects fitted very well with the overall purposes of the laboratory; others just didn't.

I told him he'd have to sit down with his young people and work toward some kind of synthesis of goals. But he should remember that he is representing an institution and that clear expectations are a very important part of an institution's climate. There have to be very clearly stated goals and standards. He has to make it clear that not all projects are compatible with the lab's goals. Those who insist on incompatible goals may have to go somewhere else to do their work.

How the large corporations will accommodate themselves to this shift in consciousness I'm honestly not sure. Perhaps there are forms of organic populism which can take place within big corporations like GE or IBM; I think that some such development will be virtually necessary if the companies want to attract the brightest and most creative of our youth. Also, there may be ways for the companies to provide cultural pluralism within their present framework; to set up minicompanies and economic boutiques which will have their own unique environments and goals within the parent company. To this end the big corporations will have to take big chances—short of destroying their markets and profit picture. So will government bureaucracies and large private but not-for-profit institutions. Because we live in a time when, even in privately owned firms, an increasingly high priority will be set on broadly social goals.

A futurist should never let himself be tempted into premature optimism. Nevertheless, I like to think we may yet develop the zeal and conscience among managers at all levels, and even among stockholders, that will produce the pressure needed to build a better environment for all of us, to make true leadership possible, and to ease the unconscionable burdens of high position.

THE IMAGE
AND
THE REALITIES

I've seen very few managers or writers on organization theory who have the courage to think in far terms, in broad-range terms, in utopian terms, in value terms.

Abraham H. Maslow, *Eupsychian Management*

Nobody can honestly think of himself as a strong character because, however successful he may be in overcoming them, he is necessarily aware of the doubts and temptations that accompany every important choice.

Dag Hammarskjöld, *Markings*

A LITTLE LOWER
THAN THE ANGELS

When I consider thy heavens, the work of thy
fingers, the moon and the stars which thou hast or-
dained;
What is man, that thou art mindful of him? . . .
For thou hast made him a little lower than the
angels, and hast crowned him with glory and honor.
Thou madest him to have dominion over the
works of thy hands; thou hast put all things under
his feet;
All sheep and oxen, yea, and the beasts of the
field;
The fowl of the air and the fish of the sea, and
whatsoever passeth through the paths of the seas.
O Lord, how excellent is thy name in all the
earth.

Psalms 8:4–9

WHENEVER I READ that phrase about the moon and the stars,
I think immediately how King David—if he could be trans-
ported from his time and place to ours—would marvel that

man could now walk on the moon and that a manmade satellite has hurtled 600 million miles into space, sending back telephotos of Jupiter from that inconceivable distance and even now is hurtling onward to become the first manmade object ever to escape entirely from the solar system. If, indeed, God gave man dominion over the works of his hands, we may now say, in pride as in humility, "What hath *man* wrought!"

In that awesome and ennobling thought, better, perhaps, that we not look down from the stars to the chaos, confusion, and carnage that man—"a little lower than the angels" —still strews about him on the good spaceship Earth. We are at a time when terrible new bloodshed has surged about King David's own ancient home, when civil war rages in Lebanon, when we have used our God-given resources so selfishly, heedlessly, and recklessly that we face crippling shortages and economic upheaval, and when a survey commissioned by the U.S. Senate shows that more than half of the American people have lost faith in their government. Surveying that dismal scene, we might well say of ourselves what Mark Twain, discussing anti-Semitism, said of the Jews: "They are members of the human race. I can't say anything worse about them."

It is in the nature of Americans to hope. André Maurois called them "in a word, optimists." I am an incurable one, and I think I'm not alone. So I'll try briefly to offer such tentative suggestions as I can; how you, I, all of us can try to become more fully human and by so doing find a reason, a future, for hope.

Each of us is, in a sense, like a miser who has vast hoards of resources and uses only a fraction of them. It is doubtful if even the greatest geniuses were ever using at any one time more than, say, 80 percent of their total potentials. Few of us are using even 50 percent. That there is a deep hunger for things we cannot find is evident in the findings of the Senate's own survey that 53 percent of Americans feel there is something "deeply wrong in America" today. What things are missing?

They are, it seems to me, chiefly these qualities: integrity — dedication — magnanimity — humility — openness — creativity. And they are equally important in leaders and in those who are led.

Let me say a bit about each one and about how we may try to meet the felt deficiency.

INTEGRITY

By *integrity* I mean standards of moral and intellectual honesty on which we base our individual conduct and from which we cannot swerve without a sense of betraying and cheapening our better selves. It is the one, single quality, I sense, whose absence we feel most sharply in every aspect of our national life. And it can only be restored by each of us asserting our own.

Every good individual strengthens society. Just *one* good person can strengthen society in ways he cannot measure. Since no man is an island, and any person's death diminishes me, so does any person's assertion of integrity strengthen my own, and yours. By their very existence, people of integrity lend new hope to our innate conviction that, as a people, we can rise above a level of moral cynicism and squalor. As Aristotle tells us in his *Ethics:* "If you would understand virtue, observe the conduct of virtuous men."

The case of Archibald Cox comes to mind. In delivering the morning prayers at Harvard recently, President Derek Bok cited the example of his former law professor in preferring dismissal to compromising the principle that ours should continue to be a government of laws and not of men. Ironically, when he left Harvard to take the post of chief special prosecutor, Cox expressed fears to Bok that his departure would set a bad example for his younger colleagues by suggesting that important government service was automatically to be preferred to the professor's chief responsibility as a teacher. "In retrospect," said Bok, "he has taught us more in government service than he could have hoped to achieve in those Harvard classrooms. . . . Few of us will face similar challenges in such dramatic forms. But all of us will surely encounter situations, however private and unheralded, that offer a similar moral challenge. By his example he has encouraged us all . . . to face them with greater strength."

The whole nation has hunted furiously for the real villains of Watergate. Yet, wherever we turn, we confront ourselves. The Watergate scandals are the ultimate sum of a million and one undiscovered, unknown, uncounted small cheatings, evasions, cover-ups, half-truths, "everybody does it" moral erosions not only in our leaders but in the whole society. Integrity, like charity, begins at home. A truly just society would need no government at all. When every individual finds and asserts a true integrity, there will be no lack of it in Washington or elsewhere.

DEDICATION

By *dedication* I mean finding something to believe in with passionate conviction and intensity. John Gardner has well said, "The best kept secret in America is that people would rather work hard for something they believe in than enjoy a pampered idleness." As I have put it, "with all the mobility, chronic churning, and unconnectedness around us, it becomes more and more important to develop some permanent and abiding commitment . . . more and more essential that we focus commitment upon a person, an institution, or an idea. This means that, as general commitments become diffuse or modified, a greater fidelity to something or someone will be necessary to make us more fully human."

What should that be? Each of us must find it for himself. But no one can live wholly and fully without having something to which he is truly dedicated and can give himself without reservation. Is it, in the present state of moral outrage, to create better government? It will not be done by signing petitions or writing Congressmen. It can be done only by going out into the vineyards of politics at the level nearest you—the precinct and ward—and exerting your own efforts to improve the structure from the bottom up. If you do, you'll be astounded at how little competition you find —and how mediocre that little will be.

There are so many needs begging for commitment, for caring. In the ghetto, for example, it is not the physical poverty that cripples children's minds so much as their deprivation of those cultural experiences we take for granted. By the age of six, this deprivation has stamped them indelibly with the conviction that all life offers anywhere is squalor, violence, addiction. If enough dedicated people cared, and tried, they could find ways to widen those horizons. How many Cincinnatians have ever visited that medieval dungeon which is the Cincinnati Workhouse? One visit alone would muster an army for prison reform.

When one dedicates oneself to something one can truly believe in, there is a joy to the work—even a sense of play—

so that, in Frost's words, there is "work and play for mortal stakes, where love and need are one." And the labor is in a real sense its own reward. As Browning writes:

> Be our joys three parts pain.
> Strive, and hold cheap the gain.

MAGNANIMITY

By *magnanimity* I mean what the dictionary says: "noble of mind and heart; generous in forgiving; above revenge or resentment."

A story in point. The tale only now is told of how, when General MacArthur failed to come out to meet President Truman's plane at their Wake Island meeting in 1950, Truman simply sat inside until he did. Then he told him: "I just want you to know I don't give a good goddam what you do or think about Harry Truman, but don't you ever again keep your Commander in Chief waiting. Is that clear?" Millions chuckle at the justified rebuke of an arrogant man.

But Lincoln, instead of sending for McClellan, called at the General's home, found him out, waited an hour with his secretary John Hay. The returning General, told that the President was waiting, simply left him waiting and sent word that he had retired. Lincoln departed, with Hay fuming at this insolence. Lincoln said, "I will hold McClellan's horse if he will bring us a victory." That was magnanimity.

HUMILITY

By *humility* I mean something very much akin to this kind of magnanimity. It is learning not to confuse your own ego and pride and self-importance with the true issue at stake. It is the ability to learn from mistakes rather than resent having mistakes pointed out. It does not mean Uriah Heepish self-abasement. It is inherent in the simplicity of every truly great man, so evident in our own time in Schweitzer and Einstein. It is Schweitzer, in his failing years, picking up a woman's heavy suitcase in Grand Central and carrying it a long way into the waiting room. It is Lincoln blacking his own boots and, when the horrified Seward cried, "Mr. Lincoln, the President doesn't black his own boots!" asking him, "Whose boots *does* he black, then?" It is John XXIII going to visit the convicts in Rome's prison, saying, "You couldn't come to me; so I came to you." It is Jesus washing the feet of his disciples. It cannot be feigned. It can be learned, but often only after a great fall of pride.

Openness

By *openness* I mean a willingness to listen to any new idea or suggestion, however seemingly bizarre. A refusal to freeze your own ideas into stereotypes and automatic litmus-paper reactions when a prejudice or preconception is challenged. A tolerance for ambiguity, an openness to change. As I suggest in *The Temporary Society*, all human relationships are likely to become more temporary, more transient. All the more need, then, in such transient and shifting relationships, to reach out for the *common humanness* of those we meet along the way. Encounter groups serve such a purpose; and increasingly, since one family in five moves every year, the transient membership of churches, as of many community endeavors, becomes an encounter group of its own. The more *depersonalized* organizational life becomes, the more each of us must seek every possible means of discovering, and developing, our own unique—and, yes, immortal—personality.

CREATIVITY

This brings me to *creativity* and to my concluding suggestion or hope: that we can find ways to develop to the fullest the wellsprings of creativity latent within us all.

It is something most of us seem to lose, or let atrophy, as we leave childhood. An artist who worked with slum children, letting them draw or paint whatever their minds suggested, concluded that every child under ten is an artist. He or she can take up pen, crayons, or water colors and create things that have the unmistakable air of distinctive originality.

The reason, of course, is that to every child the world around him is a totally new discovery, as Dylan Thomas catches perfectly in *Fern Hill:* "All the sun long it was running, it was lovely. . . . It was air and playing, lovely and watery and fire green as grass . . . the sun born over and over." The green grass, the nodding trees, the grace of animals, the poetry of wind, the grave silence of snow, the re-creating sun—all each day are born over and over. The child encounters this miracle with the sense of wonder that his elders lose as the familiarity, or tedium, of daily life shuts it out. A publisher who long dealt with great writers came to define genius thus: "Someone who sees things *very, very* clearly but sees them with the eyes of a child."

In other words, creativity is something we all have yet manage to lose. To rediscover it, we must find ways of recreating our sense of wonder, of heightening, even altering our consciousness.

We do not really see the world around us. We see only a "gloss" of stereotyped expectations. We may see a leaf but not the magic, the harmony, the incredible order of the intricate veining of a leaf.

Among students just now there is great fascination with *Journey to Ixtlan*, a serious anthropologist's story of how he spent ten years learning the secrets of an old Yaqui Indian who was, so to speak, a wizard. The wizard taught the anthropologist that he could discover what is called "a separate reality," quite different from our ordinary reality. The secret was learning to "stop the world"—to break through the gloss by which we see only what we expect to see. He who breaks the gloss can, if he stares long enough, see a whole universe in a grain of sand or a drop of water.

For centuries many have used mescaline, peyote, or other mind-altering plants to heighten consciousness, but Eastern mystics have shown that this same effect can be obtained by certain exercises or deep meditation alone. In our own country, the growing practitioners of transcendental meditation report that through some 20 minutes of quiet contemplation daily they are finding great, unsuspected powers of understanding, of serenity, of heightened wonder. Probably each of us needs to create daily some such private cathedral of contemplation.

If one reads such works as William James's *The Varieties of Religious Experience*, it seems clear that, over the centuries, many individuals have experienced a heightened consciousness that approaches a kind of illumination, that suffuses them all the rest of their lives. Whether it was Gautama Buddha or Dante, Tolstoy or Walt Whitman, all describe so much the same experience that it seems certain this illumination consists of a sudden vision, an inexpressible understanding that he or she is at one with the universe; that all life is eternal; that the sun, the rocks, the trees, the birds and fish are as much a part of him as he of them; and that all are part of one great harmonious whole. William

Blake, whose illumination transfuses both his poems and his drawings, said—and we should remember it—

You have the same intuition as I, only you do not trust or cultivate it. You can "see" what I do, if you choose.

In my specialized field, the organizational development of large management systems, it is interesting that a sub-specialty called "synectics" has developed which proves, not only that creativity can be systematically developed, but that its *organized* development can be very valuable, and profitable, in finding ingenious solutions to stubborn problems or in developing totally new products in a most imaginative way. And the key to this, just as in heightening one's consciousness, proves to be forcing oneself to see the familiar in new and different ways. It has been defined as (1) making the familiar strange and (2) making the strange familiar. It requires you, in a sense, to chop up the familiar gloss of reality into a picture puzzle, toss the pieces into the air, then reassemble them in new patterns.

Thus, it seems to me, any individual seeking to reclaim his creativity must first break the patterns of the familiar. This may be simply taking up some new interest you have long wanted to cultivate but neglected—like learning pottery, working with leaded glass, playing the piano, writing poetry or essays, bird watching, or going back, say, to the university to study fine arts at night. Developing atrophied talents. Rekindling old enthusiasms you've let die. Going for long walks. Seeing—*really* seeing—what's around you. On Cincinnati's educational station WCET René Dubos, the great scientist, expressed amazement that, standing amid all the glories of Greece, he listened to young Americans chattering about some distant place at home instead of *really seeing* what was before them.

The more our work makes us *specialists*, the more we must strive to become *generalists* in other matters, to perceive the interconnections among science, aesthetics, and ethics, to avoid becoming lopsided—like the tailor who had met the Pope and, when asked what he was like, said, "A 42 regular." Or like Darwin's gardener, who said of him, "Poor man, he just stands and stares at a yellow flower for minutes at a time. He would be far better off with something to do."

There is a beautiful interrelatedness in all the pursuits of man, whether it is science, which is essentially the pursuit of truth; aesthetics, the pursuit of beauty; or ethics, the pursuit of goodness. John Keats was criticized for being redundant, or meaningless, when he wrote, "Beauty is truth, truth beauty," yet every great scientific truth has a beauty to it, and the greatest beauty of art often has a hidden scientific truth within it.

We know, of course, that what makes the harmony of music is essentially mathematical, each higher octave of any note bearing a fixed ratio to the other of vibrations per second. Music itself is related to literary creativity. Goethe said, "It often seems to me as though an invisible genius were whispering something rhythmical to me, so that on my walks I always keep step to it, and at the same time fancy I hear soft tones accompanying some song."

For centuries, artists have used what is called "the golden rectangle" as a form of inherent beauty, using it not only as the shape of the whole painting but of objects within it. In this rectangle, the smaller side has the same ratio to the larger side that the larger has to the sum of the two sides. Its mathematical ratio is 0.38197.

Now, in mathematics there is a certain order called the

Fibonacci series that never ceases to fascinate mathematicians. It is that order—½, ⅓, ⅖, ⅜, ⁵⁄₁₃, and so on—where each successive numerator or denominator is made up of the sum of the two preceding ones.

For a long time botanists have been studying the order in which leaves arrange themselves on plants so each leaf gains unobstructed sunlight. It is called "phyllotaxy." Each arrangement of leaves ascends in a spiral. The simplest order is 180 degrees, or ½, in which every third leaf is directly above the first. The next arrangement is 120 degrees, three leaves in a cycle with a phyllotaxy of ⅓. The next order of complexity is ⅖, the next ⅜, and so on, *exactly following the Fibonacci series*. The ordering of leaves ends with the most complex arrangement possible, an angle of 137 degrees 30 minutes 28 seconds. This is known as the "ideal angle" because, at this spacing, *no* leaf will be directly over any other. Curiously enough, its mathematical ratio is 0.38197, *the same as the artist's golden rectangle*, and the ratio itself is called the golden mean.

Thus do nature and mathematics intertwine.

At first hand, one would not expect much relationship between the intuitions, say, of poets, and those of scientists. Yet the heart of poetry is, of course, metaphor—expressing one thing in terms of another ("My love is like a red, red rose")—and it is a fact often remarked that many of the great discoveries of science have come from thinking in metaphors. One of them was the Dutch physicist Kekule's discovery of how atoms lock themselves to form the benzene ring. While dozing by the fireside, he envisioned forms winding and turning like serpents, when suddenly one of the serpents swallowed its own tail. He spent the rest of the night working out how the benzene atoms were, in fact, similarly locked.

If the heightening of consciousness creates a sense of some grand, eternal unity and order to all things, it is not surprising. Not when we consider that we, the rocks, the trees, the worms are all made up of the same elemental atoms, each infinitely small and each containing within itself a tiny solar system of electrons, protons, and neutrons whirling around their own sun, the nucleus. Or that the basic life stuff itself, DNA, is the same for every living form, the same in man as in worm, their infinite forms differing only in the way these building blocks are assembled by the genetic code.

And now Pioneer 10, shooting on past Jupiter and out of the solar system entirely, sends back word to spaceship Earth that all matter is identical throughout the solar system and, presumably, the universe as well. If this sets at naught our old concepts of creation, it suggests another concept far grander and more awesome, a unity and order in life as in the cosmos, truly limitless and boundless in extent, truly world—and *worlds*—without end.

PEOPLE, CHANGE, AND THE ADAPTIVE PROCESS

CHANGE IS THE metaphysics of our age. There's no need to go into the various shock statistics people cite when they talk about the rate of change in our society, because it's the bread and butter of commencement speeches, of Sunday magazine sections, of all sorts of newspapers. We have books like *Future Shock, The Tyranny of the Transitory*, and *The Temporary Society*. The metaphors are all here.

What's really fascinating to me is how nothing seems to deter man's almost compulsive desire to unsettle, over-throw, or reject the accepted conventions and traditions. Ecclesiastes, in the Old Testament, glumly observes how man continues to disorder and unsettle his ways. It is a puzzle, because when you look beyond the recent crisis of change in our society and organizations—when you look deep down and see the human tragedies of people and organizations, you realize that's largely what life consists of these days.

I remember my first year at the State University of New York at Buffalo, where I and some of my colleagues from

East Coast and West Coast colleges had been brought in to take an upstate college into the twentieth century with a bang. I talked to a man who had something of a reputation in his field and who, I felt, was very sad about the changes that were taking place. I noticed how in the course of six or seven months he began to look like a much older man, though he was only in his midfifties. He used to walk past my office window almost daily; his shoulders seemed to get more and more stooped as each day went on. Sad affair. He confessed how unhappy he was about the new regime—how angry he felt toward the new president, because the president hadn't consulted him on a number of matters he thought he should have been consulted on. He said: "With the former president, I was in his office every day. I used to do all sorts of things for him. And I used to be called one of his 'commandos.' Now I just feel shoved aside."

Most of the book *Future Shock* is a long footnote about what I've just been observing. Yet I'm puzzled by a whole set of questions. Our organizations and institutions have to change, for all kinds of reasons. But in seeing through the crisis of change to the human and organizational tragedies— like the man with the stooped shoulders—you realize that some people are going to be hurt. It is a dilemma.

All of my education and my working life has been involved with change. I started off as an undergraduate at Antioch College, an interesting place to me for two reasons. One was its concern with public service and the application of social knowledge to influence society, opinion, and policymakers. The other was its president, Douglas McGregor, who had a great influence on me. He was one of the founding fathers of the Bethel (Maine) T-group movement, one of the pioneers in group-dynamics research and application in this country, one of the first to apply the behavioral sciences to organizational behavior and business. I became interested in small-group behavior, which led me to MIT for graduate work in an interdisciplinary program with an emphasis on social psychology. MIT was then the leading intellectual center of group-dynamics research in this country, attracting many people in psychoanalytic and social sciences who were involved in group work.

Our study of the small-group model led us to some especially interesting insights into understanding how change and innovation occur. Given a small group, social change is based on a "Truth/Love" model. The assumption behind small-group theory is that if we present enough valid data to people and develop a relationship of trust and affection and love, then change can come about. The theory relies on the idea that trust is a historical concept based on repeated interactions. That, if there's enough trust and enough truth, most changes can take place. This is in contradistinction to a model of change based on dissension, or conflict, or people operating on political, social, or economic-interest facts.

The small-group model of change also avoids situations where some people can lose. By and large, the literature in small-group theory emphasizes the consensus model, which means that nobody gets too badly hurt.

The third aspect of the small-group model is that social change tends to take place in an environmental void. Change can come from within, change agents are indigenous to the group, and the group is adaptive to cope with changes from forces within the group.

For those who create and manage change, there are many models to choose from. I have already described the "Truth/Love" model, which can also be called the "human relations" model. It relies on three things: participation of the people involved in the change, which is what most of us want; trust in the people who are the basic proponents, advocates, or leaders of the change; and, thirdly, clarity about the change. That is, what it's going to be. If those three factors aren't taken into account, tremendous mistakes occur when changes are made.

The clearer we are about what the innovation is going to be, all things being equal, the better the chance that the change will be adopted. The more participation by the people to be affected by the change, the better the chances for adoption, and for acceptance rather than limitation. The more trust in the people advocating the change, the more implementation follows.

But just to take one problem—clarity. It's very difficult to make innovations really clear. In fact, one of the most interesting things about innovation is that it's really a kind of inkblot. It's a projective screen. And it's seductive as well as projective. People can project their most anxious fantasies about it, but it also seduces interesting people into it, people who are usually of two kinds—those who are rebellious and disruptive and others who are more moderate establishment types.

There's some data from research to indicate that the human-relations model works. Unfortunately, however, it doesn't work often enough. Clarity, participation, trust—they can't always be brought into the innovation. Sometimes you have to use the *power* model.

Despite all the nice things I've said about the human-relations model, it is a fact that there has been no really basic radical restructuring of any institution by consensus. The only time restructuring of any institution has ever taken place is when someone in power has said it *will* take place. Why? Because people have a terrible time restructuring themselves when they fear that their status, their power, their esteem are going to be lowered.

Between these two extremes of the human-relations model and the power model there are other, perhaps more subtle models. At Buffalo, for example, when I set up the new nondisciplinary department of social sciences, I was only able to get away with it partly through power. It was clear that I wanted it very badly, it was clear that this was the honeymoon period of my stay there, and it was clear that I had come to Buffalo in order to set up the new department. It was also very clear that I had money from Ford. But, even with all those forces, the only way I could really get it through the faculty was by setting up the idea of a *temporary system*. And by saying: "What we're going to do is look at this program five years from now. We'll call it a program and not a department, and we'll evaluate it by certain criteria."

Part of my ulterior motive was to get the departments to evaluate themselves as well. What I really had in mind was this: "Wouldn't it be marvelous if you made all departments temporary programs?" Instead, what happened was that less than a month later the faculty made this new program a department. They were more than a little concerned with the notion of a program. So they legitimized something, partly for me and partly for their security, long before it should have been legitimized. And now it's permanent.

There's a great story about Berkeley, where in the past 10 to 15 years 88 centers have been established to function interstitially between the more formal departments. Not one of them has been terminated—with a single exception. That was a one-man center, and the man died.

We have an awesome capacity to perpetuate things long

after their reason for existence has passed. Which is why I believe in built-in rules of destruction for some situations.

My plan at Buffalo didn't work. I got the program, but I lost the principle, and I was almost more interested in the principle of temporary systems. You can restructure, but restructuring has to come from above. At Buffalo, we re-structured the whole place in such a way that you could remove lots of people from power without confronting that issue of status deprivation, or of people being fired. We removed the anxiety. Or, rather, we tended to thwart it. At least for a while.

All groups in general, but professional groups in par-ticular, do not change unless they are forced to, and they are forced to usually by three different means.

One thing that forces change is the "young Turks," which I call cabals. I have a funny distinction, which is arbitrary. I always think about organizations and change in terms of two groups: the cabals and the cliques. The cliques are in power. They have the dough, the resources; they're the establishment. The cabals are usually the younger people who are fighting the cliques. There's a high price to pay in this situation, because it really means revolution. It means that the cabals ultimately take over. Good cliques know how to co-opt cabals. They absorb protest and estab-lish a new equilibrium through a very interesting and im-portant way of politics, which is to co-opt. And, when they don't co-opt, they get into very deep trouble. One can almost do a forecast of the growth and adaptability of pro-fessional organizations on the basis of how they deal with their younger people coming up. Do they kick them out, or do they try to co-opt them?

Talk to young architects, for example. The cabals are gaining a lot of strength, and the changes in society are more or less allied with the cabals. At the same time, our systems of education do not encourage significant change, by and large. One of the big mysteries in my life is how graduate education can be basically so authoritarian and still produce people who grow up to challenge the system. How is it that these young architects, who have been trained by other architects with an older "paradigm" of what architecture is, are challenging their older colleagues to their very core? I think they're getting away with it now because society simply cannot afford to develop another generation of narcissistic architects who want to put up their own beautiful mementos. You now have to think about many people-environment interactions; you have to think about systems. You have to think about the three major deficiencies experienced in all institutions nowadays: purpose, community, and power.

Another way organizations change is through external events: the forces of society impinging on the organization. Professional groups are particularly immune to change from this source. It is very difficult to get them to redefine their professional competence, because it really seems to be a blow to their narcissism, and what you get is a guarded and defensive response.

When I was at Buffalo, I found that my department chairmen would rarely respond to any reality hitting them, except from the narrow viewpoint of their own disciplinary department. This is true of all organizations and institutions. The Army fights the Navy. But it is more severe within professional groupings. I used to kid my department chairman by reminding him of that old story of the Jew who, when he read the newspaper, would ask only one question: "Is it good or bad for the Jews?"

Change through external events is usually bad for the

"Jews." It's bad for the profession and the organization when it happens.

The third way change comes about is more profound. If I had to define what is the most important thing about change in professional and organizational life, I would answer in terms of what might be called the "culture," or the "paradigm," of a profession.

In a marvelous book called *The Structure of Scientific Revolutions*,* Thomas Kuhn wrote about how advances are made in science. His basic concept is that there's something called a "paradigm" in science, something akin to a *Zeitgeist*, or a climate of opinion which governs the choices made. Here is his definition of it: "the constellation of values and beliefs shared by the members of a scientific community that determines the choice, [the] problems which are regarded as significant, and the approaches to be adopted in attempting to solve it."

Kuhn's point is that the men who revolutionized science were always those who changed the paradigm. One of the interesting changes in paradigms today, for example, is to be seen in the social sciences: the deep concern with the conscious, introspective phenomenological aspects of personality or the subtle shift away from logical positivism toward intervention research.

The professors are saying, "The subjective consciousness is just your feeling. Let's talk about objectivity."

The students are saying, "I know what I feel." (Or, rather, "I *know* what I feel.") Their revulsion against the strategy of truth based on symbols that are both verbal and quantitative is very big. There's a real collision of these two paradigms right now, one based on the more accepted canons of science, the other based on subjective feelings.

* University of Chicago Press, 1970.

Max Weber, the sociologist, was interested in the same phenomenon. Writing about how scientific change comes about, he said: "At some time the color changes. Men become uncertain about the significance of their viewpoints, which they have used unreflectively. The path becomes lost in the dusk. The life of the great problems of culture has passed on. Then science also prepares to change its standpoint and its conceptual apparatus in order to look down from the heights of thought upon the current of events."

Paradigms—"domain assumptions," as Weber called them—they're all talking about the same thing. What is it that governs what a profession does? How does it deal with dissent in that group? What information does it use to change and adapt itself? And how do we in the professions —and in industry—identify, locate, and reward people who are *role innovators?* That is, people who don't just change the content of a particular discipline, but change its practice?

Role innovators shift the whole paradigm in a practice sense. A Ralph Nader has totally shifted a paradigm of practice about the law. When he was at Harvard Law School, he got but one course that had anything to do with consumers. And that really didn't have much to do with consumers. It was on torts, which was the closest thing to it.

Freud, of course, is a great example of a role innovator, as is a Keynes, or a Samuelson, or a Gropius. What they did was to create a new metaphor of practice in a way that was very compelling, that was not only scientifically valid but had a rhetoric and appeal that people found hard to deny.

Innovation—a new paradigm, a new way of practice, or a role innovation—has to be compelling, because preexisting theory and practice are never replaced by data disconfirming them. They are replaced only by a new theory or practice, not by studies which show that the old way no longer works.

It is not so much the articulation of goals of what a profession *should* be doing that creates a new practice. It's the imagery that creates the understanding, the compelling moral necessity that the new way is right. You have to ask, "What are the mechanisms?" It was the beautiful writing of Darwin about his travels on the *Beagle*, rather than the content of his writing, that made the difference. Because the evolutionary idea had really been in the air for a while. Not only were there parallel mentions of it, but Darwin's uncle had done some of the primary work on it. It was Freud's five cases, it's Erikson's attention to the specimen he chooses that makes all the difference. It's Kenneth Burke's "representative anecdote."

If I were to give off-the-cuff advice to anyone trying to institute change, I would say, "How clear is the metaphor? How is that understood? How much energy are you devoting to it?" Because I think it's more energy than it is courage.

Another thing I would ask is, "How well are you policing the people who give birth to what is called the 'Pinnochio' syndrome? That is, people who take your ideas and then convert them, distort them, and create real problems for you?"

Innovations are always seductive and bring in interesting people, some of whom do not, in fact, gain you adherents but instead lose them. I've always thought Branch Rickey was one of the greatest change agents. Before bringing the first black ball player into the big leagues, Rickey made sure he was impeccable, that he was the best. You can't always do this, but you must try to evaluate the embodiment of innovation in a more vigilant manner than you would when filling more orthodox positions.

In innovation, you get a sense of wanting to proselytize. The eagerness to gain adherents often leads to problems about standards. One doesn't want to be old-fashioned about it, but there is a question.

And there's another thing that worries me about innovation in the present situation. Historically, innovations have occurred during periods of economic abundance and plenty, because then the cruel collisions between two paradigms can be somehow mitigated through running parallel institutions, or through adding and increasing and expanding. It's tough when you're in a situation where you're both clamoring for the same resources. This is why I'm not sanguine right now about almost any innovation.

How do you identify and develop role innovators? How do you spot new information in institutions, organizations, professions?

I've discovered that people who are very sensitive to changes of a realistic kind are very often marginal to the institution they're a part of, almost in a geographical sense. These are the potential company "scanners" and "sensors" whose value I've mentioned before. They have useful contacts in other areas, other institutions, but they're likely to be cut off, not seen as "good organization men and women," seldom rewarded because they're viewed as mischievous troublemakers. Quite often organizations respond to them by actually reducing their rewards, in turn causing a lowered commitment, which in turn usually leads to more deviant and perhaps, finally, disruptive behavior. It's a sort of vicious cycle. Sometimes these so-called marginal people take on other jobs—which, to be realistic about it, makes them less committed to the institution. If an administrator tries to identify these people, make them his own tentacles of change, and bring them together, that's one force for inducing role innovation. I tried to do this at Buffalo, choosing people who were variance sensors yet who were viewed with some respect by their colleagues. Maybe a little bit crazy, or different, but respected. I brought these people together and used them almost as extensions of the things I was interested in.

You can also use more formal political rewards for role innovators by giving them power, money, status. It's that simple. Quite often I also brought in review boards from outside, people carefully selected in part by me, in part by the particular group affected by the innovation. This can be a useful tactic to prevent the innovator from coming into daily conflict with the resisters. It legitimizes and validates whatever changes are taking place.

With or without gimmicks like review boards, however, you can simply create a climate which allows accepted conventions to be questioned and challenged. And, by God, we'll have to, because this is exactly what's happening with the bright young people coming into these institutions right now. It's a kind of juggernaut situation. If you look at the new and the old culture, along the authoritarian-personality scale or along sociological scales, it's clear what the value differences are. A lot has to do with openness and candor versus the kind of loyalty to accepted conventions, to the kind of secrecy, which most institutions seem to use. How do we create a climate of candor and openness where we embrace error rather than aim for the safe low-risk goals that get eventual payoffs and rewards? This is especially needed in professional organizations, which are not high-risk institutions. Like the university, which, in my view, is one of the most medieval of institutions.

What I consider to be the most significant aspect of change is something like this. Organizations, by definition, are social systems where people have norms, values, shared beliefs, and paradigms of what's right and what's wrong and what's legitimate and what isn't, of how practice is conducted. One gains status and power on the basis of agreement, concurrence, and conformity with those paradigms. How can you, from within a profession, change the paradigms without being seen as too deviant or too divisively disruptive? How do you learn to evaluate information which might be interpreted as antithetical to the particular paradigm which then holds? How do you identify and reward people who continually are dissonant in the organization, who are dissident in that they are continually questioning? Not people who play devil's advocate, for I'm not in favor of establishing and legitimizing roles called "devil's advocate." I know too much of what happens to these people. You begin calling someone a devil's advocate. You listen to that person's opposing point of view—all the while feeling very self-righteous and absolving your guilt—and then you continue to do just what you did in the first place. I think of this sort of thing as the "domestication of dissent."

So how do you get role innovation, people who change practice? How do you detect signs and cues and get the right information ingested into the system? How do you develop an environment that will not squash the role innovators? Because the impulse within any paradigm is to squeeze them out, to make them leave. Their voices are too upsetting, so we ask them to exit. Or we stop listening.

How do you encourage change from within? Or do you have to take a Ralph Nader stance and attack from the outside? Is that the only way institutions can change?

When you think about the interdependence of institutions right now, when you think about the turbulence of the environment, the boundary transactions between and among organizations, and the number of technological and other kinds of changes that are forcing themselves on institutions, the question is not how we develop innovation, the question is how we are to screen and select the right alternatives. The question is this: Can we develop an organization which sees reality—not becoming faddish, spastic, other-directed, and reactive to every trend and whim that takes place—without becoming rigid, guarded, and frozen? Can we establish a pro-active, realistic organization? Obviously, if our institutions start adopting everything new, they will merely become trendy, disposable systems, with no inner core or integrity, much like an organizational counterpart to Peer Gynt.

Another great concern of mine is this: How do you communicate to people that certain changes *have* to take place—maybe even substantial changes—without creating in them *deep* resistance based on role irrelevance and incompetence and insensitivities? I'm frankly more worried, from my own experience as consultant and administrator, about the people who really fear change more than disaster. The conservative factor is always there. Where I think change-oriented people make mistakes is in thinking they're going to do away with history. That is the basic problem, because in fact most people interested in change have very ambitious hopes. They have an illusion, an omnipotent fantasy, of the clean slate. I've seen it destroyed too many times.

Every social system contains the forces for movement and the forces for conservatism—in the best sense of that word, which implies that one seeks to conserve the best and to move with some of the things one ought to move with. The point is, there are always conservative and progressive forces within every institution. One or the other of these two sides quite often tries to blot out the other, which is about as successful as blotting out one's ambivalence.

If anything, I would call myself a relentless gradualist at this point. Because I've been reading history this year, and I've been saddened to see the kind of slowness with which really basic changes in our social system take place. With all the talk about change and temporary society, I'm painfully aware of the famous crack of Crane Brinton, who said that the only thing the French Revolution brought about was the metric system. To that I should add Napoleon.

I'm saddened, also, by something else. I've had long periods of very deep concern with the fusion of theory and practice, with the hope that rationality was the only way we could ever reach anything like a civilization. And a conviction that the basic "two cultures" problem in the world is not the one that C. P. Snow has revived, between scientists and humanists, but the one between men who had knowledge and no power and men who had power and no knowledge. I kept hoping—romantically, I suppose—that somehow men who write history and men who make history would have a broadening affinity.

One of the things I felt proudest about at Buffalo was developing the new program of applied social sciences—or policy sciences—to try to shape and modify and integrate the social sciences so that they could have an impact on systems, on policy, and so on. But this was also something that caused me a good deal of concern and ambivalence. Quite often I oscillate to feelings of great despair when I realize that, probably, social knowledge is the weakest form of social influence known to man; when I realize the great difficulty of theory-practice fusion, of trying to develop knowledge that really has clout, impact on how people behave and on policy.

To return to the question of change and how you implement it—what I'm saying is that there are a variety of ways. Under which conditions you use various models has a great deal to do with the complexity and existential aspect of the group or the organization in question and its history.

It would be foolish for you as a leader to advocate any single model. I have used the power model, the human-relations model, the restructuring model, the temporary-systems model. You could also do something which I think is probably the best of anything; that is, to set up within any unit or subunit of the organization a small rotating group of people who will be called "organization renewal" people and will use the available data and ideas in order to create incremental changes.

What I think most people in institutions really want—and what status, money, and power serve as currency for—is affection, acceptance, a belief in their growth, and esteem. I think you can create changes and innovations if you succeed in not losing your affection for the people who, on the face of it, seem to be losing it. I really feel that people stay in organizations, and are satisfied in them, because they're loved and feel competent. And that we use these other things—status, money, power—as fungibles. Is there even a way of shifting some of the tangible resources and still not having that love lost? In many professional organizations it's very difficult. I would never make that statement to my department heads or deans. They would say, "Quit psychologizing—and what's all that 'love' nonsense? We're really interested in the bucks."

I don't even want to argue. I've taken an easy way out,

which is simply to use the money-and-status argument and say, "o.k., these are the levers, these are the above-the-surface counters, this is what the meter reads." But in fact it's love and esteem that count.

And so, when you want to make changes, you try to bring along with you those who perhaps have the old way of looking at things together with the new. You don't make it an either/or proposition. Nor do you try to domesticate the resisters. I've spent too much time in my life with people who cholerically defend obsolete conventions.

What is it that creates within people an identification with the adaptive process? What is it that creates a man who has a high tolerance for ambiguity? What is it that makes people throughout their lives *learning* men and women? I wish I knew. You can see it, and you can feel it, in the people who are learning as they go along. By God, I wish I knew what the personality aspects are, what the educational components were, what the developmental process is, what the family background was. I don't think we know.

But it's clear that some people—and it's not just age—continue to learn and grow throughout their lifetimes.

PERILS OF THE
BUREAUCRATIC WAY

THE REALLY STRIKING impression one gained during the
Watergate hearings was the most obvious one: how much all
the Nixon aides looked alike. I had trouble telling Dean
from Magruder, Porter from Sloan, Strachan from Haldeman. All seemed cast in the same plastic mold—young, clean-
cut, narrow-tie, radiating both a humorless purposefulness
and a numbness of moral sensibilities. In appearance, they
were almost mirror images of the younger Nixon of the
1940s, as if they were that spiritual or ghostly double called
doppelgänger.

This doppelgänger phenomenon is by no means acci-
dental, and by no means confined to the White House. If
Watergate-type cameras could zoom in on the headquar-
ters of any huge bureaucracy—government, corporation,
university, hospital—we would see it repeated more often
than we should like to imagine. By and large, people at the
top of massive organizations tend to select as key assistants
people who resemble them.

The doppelgänger effect also is independent of the
unique mentality that produced Watergate and is not
attributable *only* to President Nixon and his close asso-

ciates—meaning it would be wrong to say that, once one has examined their motivations, the matter is closed. No one can deny that they behaved in ways more reminiscent of the Keystone cops and the three stooges than of the deliberation and solemnity usually associated with the Presidency. But what I'm interested in is to show how this behavior is made explicable—though not excusable—when placed in a context of bureaucratic politics and how these politics interfere with rather than facilitate truth gathering.

Nixon is a special case in some ways. There is, in particular, his imperial view of the Presidency, which has been held by no one in the contemporary Western world except for his now deceased role model, de Gaulle. From this weird perspective his incredible position on executive privilege (repudiated only after pressure)—as if the Presidency existed on a strange planet or at least stood apart from other institutions—was as understandable as it was unreal. Nixon lacked the character or style of an extraterrestrial figure.

He didn't come off well—as a de Gaulle could. To paraphrase a famous critique of one actor's Hamlet, Nixon played king as if he were afraid someone else would play the ace.

When I was a graduate student, specializing in organizational theories and problems, I did a study showing that many leaders tended to select key assistants who resembled them, not only in ideas and attitudes, but down to such characteristics as height, stature, dress—even the cigarettes they smoked. And I learned recently that one large corporation's college recruiters have to complete the following question after each interview with a prospective employee: "Does he look like us?"

No doubt this is not to be taken too literally; the recruiter is simply asked to reflect whether, in general, the candidate seems to have the background and character that experience has shown are important to a successful career with the company. However, there *is* the danger that, in focusing too narrowly on a preferred type rather than the individual, management will fall victim to the doppelgängers.

Of course, the desire for a congenial and closely knit management group is perfectly human and, up to a point, understandable. The huge size of such organizations and the enormous overload burdening every top leader make it impossible for him to verify all his own information, analyze all his own problems, or always decide who should or should not have his ear or time. Since he must rely for much of this upon his key assistants, he would not feel comfortable in so close and vital a relationship with men who were not at least of kindred minds and of compatible personalities.

This means, inevitably, that the leader is likely to see only that highly selective information, or those carefully screened people, his key assistants decide he should see. In a very crucial situation, he may discover only too late that he has acted on information that was inadequate or inaccurate, or that he has been shielded from "troublesome" visitors who had something to tell him he should have known, or that he has been protected from some problem that should have been his primary concern. The corollary danger is that doppelgängers anxious to be more royal than the king may take actions they-feel-sure-he-wants-but-must-keep-from-him lest they either burden or, possibly, embarrass him.

The assistant is the inevitable product of the growth and scale and size of our institutions. He seems to be indispensable, although in a recent seminar with the new chairman and new president of a large life insurance company I was fascinated to learn that, while each had come to the top as "assistants to" the leader, each was now determined to get along without any and so restructure his staff and line as not to need this right-hand winnowing. I will watch with great interest to see if they can do it. For me, assistants are very useful; I cannot do without them.

The White House office has, as everybody can see, become a bureaucracy in the same sense that Max Weber meant: It has grown in size; it is characterized by specialization, division of labor, chain of command, and hierarchy. At the same time it criticizes, castigates, blames the other bureaucracy it was set up to work with. So, ironically, a minibureaucracy is established to intervene against and outside formal channels at lower and lower levels. Witness Kissinger's behavior vis-à-vis the State Department in the heyday of Nixon's minibureaucracy. This creation of the President was attempting the same kind of behavior that we all do when it gets too cold outside; its members were wrapping a warm cocoon around themselves.

Consider the rise of Presidential bureaucracy from Franklin Roosevelt's three authorized assistants to the several thousand people who worked in the executive office of Richard Nixon. The Nixon establishment included two specialized organizations for dealing with the media: one handling daily press relations and the other promotional ventures plus a new office of telecommunications policy. In addition, there was one specialized bureaucracy for dealing with foreign policy, one for domestic policy, one for national security, and so on.

During the Eisenhower and Kennedy years, the Office of the President increased 13 percent in size. Johnson increased it by a second 13 percent, and Nixon, in four and a half years, added yet another 25 percent.

If one regards a bureaucracy in its conventional stance as an organization designed to winnow information—because, after all, if one wants to deal with the blooming and buzzing confusion of the world he can do that himself—then the President's office apparatus has all the essential attributes of a bureaucracy.

It is incongruous and may be seen as pretentious to compare the problems of a university or an insurance company president to those of the President of the country. But, except for scale and magnitude, they are in many ways the same. And, if one leaves aside the questions of bugging, burglary, and the President's complicity, it can be said that we all have our doppelgängers and our Watergates. I speak, not only from experience as a consultant to organizations, but from that of four years as president of the University of Cincinnati, which, with its 36,000 students and $115 million budget, daily must meet problems comparable to those of a small city or of a sizable corporation.

Both experiences have taught me that the biggest problem of a president—any president—is getting the truth. Pierre du Pont said it well in a long-ago note to his brother Irenée: "One cannot expect to know what will happen, one can only consider himself fortunate if he can learn what *has* happened." To learn that, I must depend to a very large extent upon my vice-presidents, assistants, and staff. They are very good men and women, honest and truthful. Even so, it is not an easy matter to get full and objective truth from them.

I've always tried to be a very open person and to encourage the utmost openness and candor from all those around me. Yet time and again, after the most protracted and exhaustive meetings and discussions with these men and women, I have run into one or another of them later only to learn that some crucial question or important disagreement was not even raised.

"Why on earth didn't you talk up?" I ask. The answers I get are along these lines:

- "I didn't want to be calling you wrong in public."
- "You've got your areas, and this is one where you get very defensive."
- "I thought I'd catch you alone outside last week, but I never got around to it."
- "I didn't think I would win the argument against you, despite the fact that I felt you were making a mistake."
- "I didn't want to burden you by dropping another load on your shoulders."

Yet it may be precisely a burden that *should* be on my shoulders.

Much is made of that final responsibility "The buck stops here." However, a president is often lucky if he can find the buck at all, learn where it stopped, or discover who stopped it before it reached him. I wish I could get more genuine "bucks" on my desk, rather than the myriad of frittering detail that does get dumped there so that (what I have phrased as Bennis's law) routine work drives out the important.

People in power have to work very hard on getting people to tell them the truth. The right people will, and the right bosses will hear it.

The whole Vietnam mess, which almost wrecked the country, grew out of people's not telling the truth, failing to tell what they did know, or lacking the courage to act in situations they knew to be wrong. The deliberate faking of air mission reports in the 1969 and 1970 "secret" bombing of Cambodia is only one instance of official lying to emerge. More subtle is concealment by inaction. Even George Ball, that prophet with most honor for his internal predictions of where the fatal chain of actions would lead, never let the public itself in on his dismay. This he justified later by saying, "After all, we're just hired hands of the President."

In the 1960s, when I made some organizational studies for the State Department, I quickly learned that junior foreign service officers (FSOs) often decided not to tell their bosses what they knew from the field situation because they believed the bosses would not accept it, only to learn later that the boss felt the same way but in turn kept silent for fear *his* boss would disapprove. Up and down the line, this went on to the very top. Each privately knowing what was right, all enclosed themselves in a pluralistic ignorance, much like the husband who doesn't want to go to a movie but thinks his wife does, and whose wife doesn't want to go but thinks *he* does, so that both do go though neither wanted to.

This situation gives point to Khrushchev's answer to one of the anonymous written questions handed up to him at a New York press conference. The question: What was he, an important figure, doing during all those crimes of Stalin he had retroactively exposed and denounced? Khrushchev was livid with rage. "Who asked that question?" he demanded. "Let him stand up!" Nobody did. "That's what I was doing," said Khrushchev.

As in all bureaucracies, people in the State Department practice a terrible oversimplification process. There is no time for them to see things in a complex, differentiated, dialectical way. This helps them keep their distance; by reducing men and women to stereotypes they eliminate the need to learn from them. The State Department was trying to get its administrative officers to learn more about the Foreign Service, and the FSOs to learn more about administration. Both tried to avoid this, the administrators by reducing the envoys to the stereotype of "pin-striped, cookie-pushing snobs," the FSOs by reducing administrators to uncultured "car-pool supervisors."

In the same manner the staff around a president develops stereotypes about people: "The boss wouldn't want to see him—he's the fellow who went to the wedding in tennis shoes." The president himself may say, "Jesus, did you see what So-and-So told the *Post?*" and down through assistant through secretary to people taking down phone calls, go reverberations felt miles away even when they're quite unreal. So suddenly a very few people are implicitly skewing, selecting information that gives you an inaccurate picture on which decisions may be based. Such skewedness can affect history: Barbara Tuchman in her book on China tells how, in the 1940s, Mao Tse-tung wanted very much to visit Roosevelt, but Roosevelt canceled the proposed meeting on the basis of incredibly biased information from Ambassador Pat Hurley. It was nearly 30 years later that another President sought out the meeting with Mao which, had it taken place earlier, conceivably could have averted many subsequent disasters.

I have chosen, for my own principal assistants, people who have faculty tenure—for the simple reason that, since they have something to go back to if either of us doesn't like the relationship or find its results satisfactory, they are much freer to be outspoken and to try to give me the objective truth. At the same time, since they come from a constituency—the faculty—they know what is practical and possible in dealing with its problems, but being away from that constituency also enables them to approach these problems more objectively. I tell them I plan to rotate them frequently—so that no one will spend more than one or two years as an assistant—both to keep them fresh and to preclude their becoming preoccupied with a personal vested position.

This objectivity is imperative because everyone else who reports to you—deans in my case or Cabinet officers in the case of the President—does represent a constituency and simply because of this cannot give you objective, unbiased advice.

A beautiful example of this happened when I promoted one of my ablest assistants to a top academic post. Only a month before, he had argued with me most persuasively that my notion of using a faculty member as a half-time assistant just would not work. Now, when I told him I had in mind choosing an academic department head as his replacement, he urged that the man act as my assistant only half-time while continuing to head his department. He gave very good and cogent reasons as to why his views on half-time work had shifted 180 degrees in a single month, but what had really changed was that he was now speaking from a constituency, and with very different concerns.

A president's assistant should give him complete loyalty. The problem is that if he is your person, and *only* your person, he has a personal stake in his continuation in that role and for that reason he may, unconsciously, not tell you the whole truth. It is the vulnerability that comes from being totally dependent on one person.

If it is not absurd to transpose the lessons of my own experience to former President Nixon's much-debated problems, these latter seem to me to have stemmed in considerable part from the fact that his Orange County doppel-gängers were in precisely that position of vulnerability. None had ever been elected to any office and thus had little or no concept of what was politically realistic and what was politically dangerous, perhaps even mortally so. Having no previous constituency, none had anything to fall back upon, and all were completely dependent on the approval or disapproval of one man. As we have seen, this skewed, not only the information they got and gave, but also their personal concepts of what was ethically, morally, or legally permissible. Whatever responsibility the President may have had for the mess he ended in, there is no question that his own doppelgängers helped put him there. As a French saying has it, "It was worse than a crime; it was a blunder."

How can future Presidents avoid such humiliation and entrapment by overeager "spiritual and ghostly doubles"? To this end I would urge:

1. *As much as possible, he should put his key assistants on temporary duty*, at most for two years, with the advance knowledge that they will be rotated. This will make them less likely to overreach in the effort to consolidate their own power positions. It will make for less arrogance, greater humility, more openness to countervailing ideas and counsel. It will also diminish the interesting need *not* to know that seemed to characterize Nixon's doppelgängers and was reflected so well in the kinds of remarks we heard about on the tube:

Colson to Hunt: "Don't tell me."

Ehrlichman to Sloan: "I don't want to know."

2. *He should see that some, not all, of his assistants have at some time had relationships with some important con-*

stituency. They should then know the limits of politics and the limits of power. Obviously, neither Haldeman nor Ehrlichman had the faintest idea about either. Melvin Laird, former Congressman, had; so did ex-Governor Connally.

3. *He should run, not walk, from the doppelgänger syndrome.* If a President is, like Nixon, naturally reclusive, he should not surround himself with men who are even more so. He should seek to surround himself with the utmost diversity of view still capable of being orchestrated harmoniously. I don't mean that he should bring in revolutionaries or radicals, or even devil's advocates. He does need people who are different from each other in experience, attitude, approaches, and philosophies.

4. *He ought to read at least one daily newspaper.* A man who relies for his news on a daily summary, preselected and tailored by doppelgängers eager to provide him with what they think he is eager to hear, may not discover the truth until long after the whole nation knows it. Far from assuming that a person is out to "get" him, he could do worse than heed a wise old editor's credo that the best maxim for a good reporter is this: "Beware of finding what you're looking for." A President who hears only what he wants to hear, and finds only what he wants to find, will find himself in trouble.

5. *Finally—to make one thing perfectly clear—he cannot rely exclusively on his palace guard for information.* Hard as it is to do so, he must remain accessible, despite the fact that accessibility in modern times seems one of the most underrated of political virtues. In his Watergate testimony, I recall Haldeman sounding generally unrepentant about the "tight ship" he ran at the White House. Unquestionably, Mr. Nixon's inaccessibility was due to his per-

sonal inclinations as well as Mr. Haldeman's "Berlin wall," but his attitude suggested that the lesson of Watergate had still not sunk in.

The Romans, who were the greatest politicians of antiquity, and probably also the busiest men, valued the quality of accessibility highly in their leaders. Cicero, in praising Pompey, commented on his ready availability, not only to his subordinates, but to the ordinary soldiers in his command.

A later Roman historian recounted this even more telling anecdote about the Emperor Hadrian: The emperor, who at that time ruled almost the entire civilized world, was riding into Rome in his chariot when an old woman blocked his path. The woman asked him to hear a grievance. Hadrian brushed her aside, saying he was too busy. "Then you're too busy to be emperor!" she called after him. Whereupon he halted his chariot and heard her out.

I would offer much the same suggestions to the president of any large organization. Today we are *all* organization men and women. Where 75 years ago, only 10 percent of our people worked for what Berle and Means called an organization and 90 percent were self-employed, today the ratio is just the reverse. Every pebble dropped in Watergate has had its ripples throughout our complex organizational society, and by the same token it is the excesses, the concealments, the arrogances and half-truths of a thousand faceless doppelgängers, in innumerable large organizations, that make a Watergate possible.

My favorite E. M. Forster passage, in *Howard's End*, is this: *"Only connect."* It is easy enough to cry shame on Watergate without perceiving its interconnections with our own lives and organizations and, in lesser degree, our conduct. *The New York Times*, in publishing the Pentagon

Papers, thundered at the Pentagon bureaucracy without pausing to reflect that it has a bureaucracy of its own which in many ways might be a microcosm of the other.

So let us indeed be angry about Watergate.

Let us also connect.

MEET ME
IN MACY'S WINDOW

THE BRITISH FOREIGN OFFICE gives its fledgling diplomats three cardinal rules of behavior: (1) never tell a lie, (2) never tell the whole truth, and (3) never miss a chance to go to the bathroom. An old Tammany boodler, who disliked leaving any traces of his dealings, had a terser rule: "Don't write. Send word."

Both sets of rules, I fear, are likely to become more and more a tacit standard of conduct for those who, in the post-Watergate climate of suspicion, share the hazardous privilege of running large organizations, including, in my own case, the nation's second largest urban multiversity.

Never have the American people felt such universal distrust of their presumed leaders, whether in government, the law, the clergy, or education. Year after year of calculated deception over Vietnam, compounded by the conspiracy, skullduggery, and chicanery of Watergate, have left them trusting almost no one in authority.

Consider a recent Gallup survey in which college students were asked to rate the honesty and ethical standards of various groups: political officeholders (only 9 percent rated "very high") were eclipsed only by advertising men

(6 percent), lawyers rated 40 percent, journalists 49 percent. I am proud that college teachers rated highest (70 percent), but since college presidents were not included, I can't seek shelter under that umbrella. Ralph Nader got a higher rating than President Ford, Henry Kissinger, or Ted Kennedy. Labor leaders came out even worse than business executives—19 percent and 20 percent respectively.

In short, virtually all leaders are in the doghouse of suspicion. And the understandable reaction to all these credibility gaps is creating a growing insistence that every public act, of whatever public institution, be conducted, as it were, in Macy's window.

Some symptoms:

• "Sunshine laws" have now been passed by numerous states prohibiting closed meetings. Hawaii has even made it a crime to hold a private meeting of *any* sort without giving advance notice.

• The Buckley Amendment requires that all records in institutions with federal support (particularly those concerning students) be open to inspection by the person concerned.

• The Freedom of Information Act, first passed in 1967 and recently strengthened over the President's veto by amendments that became effective February 19, 1975, requires that most records of federal agencies be provided to anyone upon request.

The intended purpose of all such measures is wholesome. It is to create a standard, for all public business, of what Wilson called "open covenants openly arrived at." I believe wholeheartedly in such a purpose. Over many years of consulting, teaching, and writing on the achievement of organizational goals (for all organizations, but particularly those of business and government), I have always stressed the importance of openness.

I have argued that goals will be achieved effectively almost in proportion to the extent that the organization can achieve a climate where members can level with one another in open and trusting interpersonal relationships. I believe this, because denial, avoidance, or suppression of truth will ultimately flaw the decision making. In the case of business, the bottom line will be affected as well.

So—I dislike secrecy. I think the prophet Luke was right when he wrote, "Nothing is secret, that shall not be made manifest." I believe Emerson's law of compensation: "In the end, every secret is told, every crime is punished, every virtue rewarded, in silence and certainty."

At the same time I am convinced, as a practical administrator, that these well-intended goldfish-bowl rules will have unintended results worse than the evils they seek to forestall. They are likely to produce more secrecy, not less (only more carefully concealed), and on top of it, so hamstring already overburdened administrators as to throw their tasks into deeper confusion.

For secrecy is one thing; confidentiality is another. No organization can function effectively without certain amounts of confidentiality in the proposals, steps, and discussions leading up to its decisions—which decisions should then, of course, be open, and generally will be.

An amusing case in point. The Nixon government moved heaven and earth seeking to restrain *New York Times* editors from publishing the Pentagon Papers, perhaps even by imprisonment. The *Times* won the right from the Supreme Court (under some continuing criminal risk) to resume publishing these assertedly "secret" studies of

Vietnam War decisions. Yet the editors themselves surrounded their preparation of these stories with a secrecy and security the Pentagon might envy—renting a secret suite of hotel rooms, swearing each member of a small secret staff to total secrecy, confining them for weeks almost like prisoners, restricting their communications to an elite handful with the "need to know," and setting the stories themselves on sequestered, closely guarded typesetting machines. Thus the ultimate challenge to "official" secrecy was performed in ultimate "private" secrecy.

What the *Times* editors knew, of course, was what every decision maker knows instinctively. The mere fact of discussions becoming known at the wrong stage of the procedure can prevent a desirable decision from ultimately being carried out.

We have seen this happen in the case of the long, arduous, confidential negotiations Secretary of State Kissinger was making with the Soviets to tie trade concessions to larger, mutually agreed quotas of emigration for Soviet Jews.

He had already obtained, through quiet negotiation, large but unstipulated expansions of the actual numbers of emigrés, who began arriving in Israel by the thousands. He obtained similar agreement to larger expansions. But zealous Senatorial advocates of larger emigration demanded that all this be put in Macy's window—that it be publicly recorded, and that the Soviets publicly confirm what they were privately conceding. The outcome was to upset détente itself and the progress already gained in emigration.

On a less global level, some experiences of my own bring home how vital confidentiality can be in determining whether or not ultimately "open decisions openly arrived at" can be made at all.

Case 1. Shortly after I became president of the University of Cincinnati, of which the city's largest hospital (General) is a part, a U.S. Senator announced an investigation of whether whole-body radiation, carried out at General on terminal cancer patients, constituted "using human beings as guinea pigs." The charges were totally false, but there were some awkward aspects of the way the whole thing had been handled which caused me to investigate the reasons privately.

This was on the eve of a Hamilton County election absolutely crucial to the hospital, on which thousands of the poor rely for treatment. It was far from sure whether a major bond levy for General Hospital would pass or fail. It did pass, but during three critical weeks I had either to evade all questions relating to my own and to the Senator's investigation or fudge my answers. I never lied. I never told the whole truth. I often went to the bathroom.

Case 2. Our university, which began as a city-funded municipal college and to which the City of Cincinnati still contributes $4.5 million of its annual $140 million budget, now draws the bulk of its funding from the state. But it is not a full state institution like Ohio State. If we *were* fully state affiliated, we would receive sufficient extra funds to meet a worsening financial crisis. The possibility of such affiliation therefore not only *needs* to be considered but *has* to be considered.

But if we were to seek full state status, timing would be very important, since it would involve not only action by the legislature but a change in the city's charter. Even more important, I learned to my sorrow, was confidentiality.

One of our state senators, preparing for a TV interview, asked me if it was all right for him to say that the University was "considering" such a move. I said, "Certainly," since obviously I had to consider it. By night this statement of the obvious was "big" news flashing across my TV screen. By morning local and state politicians were making a pro-and-con beanbag of the question, and by then the furor was such that it was difficult even to weigh or discuss the problem on its merits. Happily, that frenetic period has now passed and the question is being calmly and thoughtfully debated—but I learned a lesson.

Case 3. Last year a group of black graduate students made charges of "racism" against their college faculty. I met with this group and heard out their grievances. I told them that if the faculty would agree, I would ask a blue-ribbon panel of distinguished local citizens, including two black leaders, to investigate and report on the matter.

That was Wednesday. On the next day, Thursday, the Dean of the College had arranged to meet with the faculty. The plan was to make this proposal for such a committee. I had no reason to think the faculty would object.

But by late that Wednesday afternoon the Cincinnati *Post* was blazoning the entire story—the protest meeting, my proposal to the blacks, tomorrow's meeting arranged with the faculty, etc. Obviously, the protesters had "leaked" the details of our meeting, apparently assuming it would further their cause. The opposite happened. The faculty members were irritated by reading about arrangements they had not been consulted about. By the time I *could* consult them, they were sufficiently angry to vote down the whole proposal of an outside committee. Werner Heisenberg's "uncertainty principle" affects human as well as molecular relations: the mere act of observing a process (publicly) *can impede the process itself.*

So—it is certainly clear in my own mind that there are times when confidentiality is a necessary prerequisite to *public* decisions for the *public* benefit. But when one asks, or is asked, where this desirable good blends into the undesirable evil of secrecy—for secrecy's own sake, or for concealing mistakes—it is hard to set any very clear or definitive standards or rules of thumb.

One almost has to come back always to the character, the integrity, of the individual concerned. If the person is worthy of trust, his judgment must be trusted as to when, and under what circumstances, confidentiality is required.

Unquestionably, however, certain individuals are by nature so obsessed with secrecy and concealment one suspects that, as infants, they were given to hiding their feces from their parents. One thinks immediately of Nixon. His former speechwriter, William Safire, reveals in his book, *After the Fall*, that Nixon was so secretive that, prior to his election, he mistrusted even the Secret Service men guarding him. Richard Allen, his foreign policy adviser, wanted to bring him together with Anna Chennault, widow of the Flying Tiger general, who was pulling strings to block a Johnson bombing pause in North Vietnam. "Meeting would have to be absolute top secret," wrote Allen to "DC" (Nixon's "code" name). Secretive old "DC" scribbled opposite this reference to top secret,

Should be but I don't see how—with the S.S. [Secret Service] If it can be [secret] RN would like to see—if not—could Allen see for RN?"

Note that, for extra secrecy, he even writes of himself in the third person: DC, even to himself, is RN.

We all know where this excessive passion for secrecy led. Kissinger not only had Safire's phone tapped, but even recorded—without their knowledge—conversations with such co-equals as budget director George Shultz. Writes Safire:

This tolerance of eavesdropping was the first step down the Watergate road. It led to eavesdropping by the plumbers, to attempted eavesdropping on the Democratic National Committee, and to the ultimately maniacal eavesdropping by the President, on the President, for the President, completing the circle and ensuring retribution. Eavesdropping to protect Presidential confidentiality led to the greatest hemorrhage of confidentiality in American history and to the ruination of many good men.

Indeed, I sometimes think it is such *needless* passion for secrecy in many of our institutions, corporate as well as governmental, that has set off the present demand to wash, as it were, all public information in Macy's window. It has set off, as well, the unprecedented epidemic of public litigiousness, where every leader of any institution now has to consult his lawyer about even the most trivial decisions. (I am currently involved in so many lawsuits my mother now calls me "My son the defendant.")

So even while I defend the need for confidentiality, I argue for the utmost possible openness—for "leveling"—in every institutional hierarchy. This leaves us with a paradox. The more we can establish *internal* truth—true openness, true candor, true leveling—within an organization and its hierarchy, the better able it will be to define, and defend, the proper areas of *external* confidentiality. Once a business executive is convinced that the enemy is not across the hall but across the street, the less inclined he will be, so to speak, to hide his feces.

Nevertheless, the national mania for "full information" is very much with us, and is now part of the turbulent social environment that every administrator must deal with. Dealing with it wisely will challenge all his tolerance for ambiguity. Freud's definition of maturity was the ability to accept and deal with ambiguity.

Among colleges, one result is already clear. The Buckley Amendment is laudable in its intent, but henceforth school and college administrators are going to be chary of putting any very substantive information into any student's record. What will wind up there will be so bland and general as to perhaps be useless to college-entrance officials in making a considered judgment of an applicant's overall merits. If, for example, he had threatened to cut a teacher's throat but not done so, he could scarcely be described as "Possibly unstable"—the student or his parents might sue.

Edward Levi, the new attorney general who was the dean of Chicago's law school and president of the university, is able to see these problems from all those perspectives. As a respected civil libertarian, he has publicly exposed flagrant abuses by the FBI's late Director J. Edgar Hoover—most notably an asinine "Cointel" game of sending anonymous letters to both Mafia and Communist leaders with the intent to stir up conflict between them. At the same time, Attorney General Levi has stressed the necessity of confidentiality, not only for government but private groups and citizens. As for Wilson's famed "open covenants," Levi quotes Lord Devlin: "What Wilson meant to say was that international agreements should be published; he did not mean that they should be negotiated in public."

In government, the Macy's window syndrome is going to make for greater inefficiency, because officials are going to spend more and more of their time processing requests for documents on *past* actions instead of applying the same energy to *future* actions. Levi points out that the FBI, which received 447 "freedom of information" requests in *all* of 1974, this year received 483 requests *in March alone.* "As of March 31, compliance with outstanding requests would require disclosure of more than 765,000 pages from Bureau files."

Such demands can, it seems, be self-defeating. One suit to compel disclosure of Secretary Kissinger's off-record briefing on the 1974 Vladivostok nuclear arms negotiations yielded 57 pages of transcript, but three pages were withheld on grounds that "attribution to Mr. Kissinger could damage national security." More important, it raised the question of whether any future briefings would be equally informative—or, in some cases, discontinued entirely. As the Supreme Court observed, even while denying President Nixon's right to withhold the crucial Watergate tapes: "Human experience teaches that those who expect public dissemination of their remarks may well temper candor with a concern for appearances and for their own interests to the detriment of the decision-making process."

In the case of meetings of public bodies—school boards, college regents, and the like—the disclosure mania will make for more and more cliques which meet privately beforehand to agree on concerted actions subsequently revealed only at the "public" meeting. What is likely to emerge are the "pre-meeting-meetings" novelist Shepherd Mead described in ad agency conferences in his *The Great Ball of Wax.*

In every important decision that is apt to impinge on this new "right to know," there will very likely be far fewer written, recorded discussions, far more private, oral discussions, far more tacit rather than "official" decisions. And more winks than signatures ("Don't write; send word") if for no other reason than to avoid some new capricious lawsuit.

The public will be learning more and more about things of less and less importance. It will be poorer served by administrators trying to fight their way through irrelevant demands for "full information" about old business, to the neglect of attending to new business.

I am not saying that individuals who have been unjustly accused should not be able, as Freedom of Information provides, to examine their own dossiers. Nor am I saying it is unwholesome for any government or public agency to be prodded out of its passion for hiding its mistakes under "classified" labels. That kind of file cleaning and purging is needed. Furthermore, scholars are finding the law a great boon in gaining quicker access to needed documents and archives.

What I *am* saying is that in the long run we are likely to get better government, better decisions, by focusing our energies on finding leaders whose innate integrity, honesty, and openness will make it unnecessary for us to sue them or ransack their files later on. Ed Levi, it seems to me, cuts to the heart of the dilemma:

A right of complete confidentiality in government could not only produce a dangerous public ignorance but also destroy the basic representative function of government. But a duty of complete disclosure would render impossible the effective operation of government.

LEADER POWER
IN AN EXPLOSIVE
ENVIRONMENT

THE CONSPICUOUS ABSENCE of real leadership throughout today's world calls to mind the story of the Frenchman who was bowled over and all but trampled by a noisy, unruly mob that was swarming down the street. As he crawled gingerly to his feet, he confronted a small, inoffensive-looking man who was frantically running after the crowd.

Wishing to save a fellow human being from similar harm, the Frenchman cried in warning: "Don't follow those people!"

"I *have* to follow them!" yelled the little man over his shoulder. "I'm their leader!"

People without leadership, leaders who follow. Yet the more we lack for leadership, the more we hunger for it. Bewildered, we wander through a world that seems to have become morally dead, where everything, including the government, seems up for sale and where, looking for the real villain of Watergate, we confront everywhere ourselves.

"Each of us," Thomas Wolfe writes, "is the sum of all the things he has not counted."

And the thing we have come to call by the name of Watergate is the sum of a thousand smaller, unknown Watergates. Every assistant in the White House who failed to tell his boss the things he knew the boss would not really want to know has his counterpart in a thousand other bureaucracies—including universities and giant industrial enterprises. Watergate was not the evil doing of a handful of men, though evil indeed it was. It is the sum of all the things we have not counted, the betrayal of values, once taken for granted, at the hands of all the men and women who wield the power in our society. In Walt Kelly's unforgettable words, "We have met the enemy—and he is us."

If we have no leaders worthy to be so regarded by us, it is not their failure but ours. Many of us are leaders too, or *called* leaders, and when leadership is lacking below, it cannot be expected at higher levels. So let us ask ourselves:

What is preventing us from being leaders, *true* leaders?
What are the obstacles that we must overcome?
What are the true tasks of leaders?
How can we achieve them in a turbulent, unstable world?

I shall venture some tentative answers, well aware that there can be no certitude in times like these. As Oliver Wendell Holmes said, "Certainty generally is illusion, and repose is not the destiny of man." And such answers as I do offer come, in a sense, from a head wearing two hats that sometimes mock one another by facing in opposite directions.

One hat is that of the man who has spent most of his adult life as a student of management practice and organizational behavior and as a theorist of better organizational development—in short, leadership. As the No. 2 man of the University of Buffalo for three years and the No. 1 man of the University of Cincinnati for four, I have suffered that worst of all fates of leadership theorists—the fate of having a leader's hat clapped on one's head and being told, "Okay, you told 'em how to do it. Now *show* 'em."

Well, I've kept a sort of double-entry ledger at both places, putting down in one column the specific theories I wanted to apply to my problems and, in the other, noting how they really worked out in practice. The experience has been painful, and I will only say there is nothing like the firing line to strain an armchair general's strategy—not to mention the chair or the seat, too, for that matter.

But what is it that prevents me from being as good a leader as I want to be? The biggest obstacle, of course, for you as well as for me, is the turbulent, unstable world. It is the explosively changing environment in which we have to function.

Within the past quarter-century, change has become the only constant, bringing jet planes, computers, missiles, satellites, space travel, thermonuclear power—and terror. In Paris around 1900, Henry Adams, observing that each decade since 1870 had seen a doubling of the energy extracted from a ton of coal, foresaw that the century ahead would bring such exponential acceleration of electrical, chemical, and radiating energy as to give man power that should make him the equivalent of a god. He saw it, also, as if man were being threshed about by a live wire that he couldn't let go.

Yet consider how Adams's perceived "law of acceleration" has itself accelerated. In the past hundred years we have increased our communication by a factor of ten to the seventh power, our speed of travel by ten squared, our speed of data handling by ten to the sixth power, our energy resources by ten to the third power, our power of weapons by ten to the sixth power, our ability to control diseases by ten squared, our rate of population growth by ten to the third power.

The modern leader is inundated, is buried by such an avalanche of information that in physics alone J. Robert Oppenheimer waggishly estimated that, if the new information continued its rate of growth, the *Physical Review*, a leading journal, would by the year 2000 weigh more than the earth. Getting, handling, and interpreting information is now the dominant business of our whole economy, so much so that, when the Xerox breaks down, our entire organization also breaks down.

Yet, even as the world itself has shrunk to a global village, our own society has split itself into so many different segments, fragments, and caucuses that the old ideal of consensual government has become impossible. It was Lyndon Johnson's tragedy to ask with Isaiah, "Come, let us reason together," at a time when all these fragmented segments scarcely wanted to *be* together, let alone reason together.

We saw Black Panthers in America and White Panthers in Jerusalem, Women's Lib and Gay Lib, drug culture and rock culture, draft avoiders and divorcees, parents without children, children without parents. At our University of Cincinnati campus alone we have over 500 various governance and interest groups—so many that one can scarcely keep track of them, much less find time to meet with them very often.

All these splinters, these caucuses, have nothing in common save one thing—all regard themselves as oppressed and subjugated, and all share an unbridled desire to rise even if, sometimes, at the expense of the others. The Peruvians have a word for this—*arribismo*. The French say *arrivisme* and the Italians *arrivismo*, and both mean "pushiness." But the Peruvians, when they say it, mean something sharply more. They mean, "You've got yours, Jack, and by God I'm going to get mine!" It's an explosive *arrivisme*, not a social-climbing one. It's not what Norman Podhoretz means by "making it."

The U.S. *arribismo* distinguishes all these Americans of different groups, trying to find their identity along race lines, sex lines, ethnic lines, or even age lines; who are at different stages of their social identity and their economic and political power.

They are telling us that the old dream of the melting pot, of assimilation, does not work and hasn't been working. They've never been "*beyond* the melting pot" as Moynihan and Glazer saw it; they've been *behind* it. And they say, "Nuts to the American dream and shibboleth of 'Work hard and get ahead, and you'll become part of the mainstream of America.'" They say, "No. We don't *want* to be part of the mainstream."

And, since our country has always been based on merit and achievement, and the work ethic has been the stem-winder of our society, this makes leadership—any form of it—very complex and difficult, full of moral dilemmas and shifting values. It is a fragmentation yet an interdependent mosaic.

Our campuses, like our capital, are no longer torn by Vietnam; and the Cold War is giving place to détente. Optimists have long hoped that the American and Soviet societies may gradually converge, yet it may be that both have already converged more than either would like. Hugh

Sidey told me that when Kissinger was working out the details of Nixon's Moscow visits, both his bureaucrats and their Soviet opposite numbers were amazed at how much they thought and worked alike.

The Soviets are now persecuting the father of their H-bomb (just as Lewis Straus persecuted Oppenheimer), and our buggers and burglars seem both so familiar and so unexceptionable to their Soviet counterparts that they do not report, much less deplore, their activities.

Moreover, as the confrontation of the one society with the other diminishes, each now begins a new confrontation with itself, and the new test is which can best resist the forces of internal disintegration that eat away at both. Instead of peaceful coexistence, it could be called "competitive decadence," less to increase one's comparative power than decrease one's comparative vulnerability; to encourage, as France's Pierre Hassner puts it, "exported erosion."

Along with internal erosion and the loss of consensus has come the loss of community, of comity—and power. Almost every leader I talk to, of any institution, expresses a sense of powerlessness, a loss of autonomy and independence.

If you consider the placid business environment of 1900 or even 1925, when both labor and raw materials were scooped up wherever you found them, just as from one amorphous pool, and when both taxes and government regulations were comparatively light, you see today's world as one where the power of decision is increasingly circumscribed and limited, by internal and by external forces.

The businessman's freedom of decision is increasingly limited, on the one hand, by powerful unions and, on the other, by unpredictable incursions by government bureaus, by administrative fiat, by sometimes capricious legislation,

and—with the enormous growth of multinational corporations—by the unforeseeable disruptions of a punitive law in
France, an increased English corporate tax, a war in the
Middle East, or even an Arab shutdown of world oil. Sheer
chance, as much as conscious planning, rules the affairs of
men.

In the case of our university, I must not only balance
the interests and demands of all these constituencies I have
mentioned but pay equal or more attention to the City
Council, the State Legislature, Supreme Court edicts, political movements, the Governor, and what the Federal Government may or may not do for education. All those major
changes that have completely transformed the university—
Sputnik, the population explosion, the draft, affluence, you
name it—have come from the outside; yet most of us share
a self-concept that we still live in an Oxbridge, a walled
cloister, a citadel several terrain features from "the action."
I will hear: "Oh, my God, let's not cheapen ourselves with
lobbying!" We eschew the idea of student "markets" despite the fact that we have become increasingly tuition-
dependent, and we find that the thought of making our
catalog attractive suggests the heinous taint of Madison
Avenue.

If the legislature demands that our medical school admit
a certain proportion of Ohio citizens, up goes the flag of
academic freedom (I have argued that position personally),
up goes the cry of "Let's not let these damned politicians
dictate our admissions programs." The fact is that our medical school is taking 120 people out of 8,000 applicants at a
time when everybody wants to be a doctor, or a lawyer,
and when jobs after college aren't all that secure. We're
making political and economic decisions when we tell 7,880
families they cannot guarantee a good, steady income for

their sons and daughters. So, yes—let's have academic freedom. But let's not be surprised when the people concerned make their own political decisions, through the legislature, about admissions.

The Tides of Change

Not only is our environment changing, but so are the nature of our work and thus the components of our economy. For the first time, services of all kinds, including education, now account for a larger proportion of our gross national product than does industry. And the fastest-growing services are those provided by state and county governments. This area includes health and welfare services as well as education; it now accounts for 80 percent of the total nationally, and is growing. The fastest-growing union in the United States is the municipal workers union.

When the voters of Ohio approved an income tax for the first time, effective in 1972, a tremendous campaign was waged for it. Yet, in my opinion, it was voted in, not so much because of this campaign, as because so many of the voters—dependent on the public payroll—realized that their own economic integrity depended on it.

Where the demands of unions were once chiefly bread-and-butter issues, today the unions are becoming concerned with the *climate* of work, with opportunities for learning, with conditions that enhance the individual's personal life and human dignity. Such changes are desirable, and good for the whole society. But they unquestionably narrow, more and more, what were once wholly management prerogatives. Management's power diminishes.

And with that has come a loss of credibility, and trust,

in institutions as a whole, in leaders as a whole. This was true *before* Watergate.

Time was, for example, when 65 percent or so of the public felt that it could trust the newspaper editor. His credibility is still one of the highest, but it is now more like 28 percent than 65.

Not even the most revered institutions are immune. Recently a lead article in *The Wall Street Journal* described a national wave of distrust toward the Canadian Mounties, which, under the Hollywood influence, I always thought of as a group of the most impeccable, clean-cut Nelson Eddys. At most, they might have stolen a kiss in a movie from Jeanette MacDonald. Now they are suspected of stealing a lot more, and of drunkenness and brutality as well.

The movies also used to give us such strong, silent heroes as Gary Cooper and Spencer Tracy. Now, with the exception of Patton, they give us for the most part anti-heroes, antileaders. Yet the young hunger for leaders, with a fierce and highly moral force. If God is dead (the churches are shrinking), Christ is not. He is the archetypal leader for thousands of the young, and there are now likely more Christians outside the churches than within them.

The once monolithic Roman church has, since Pope John's aggiornamento, erupted in startlingly liberal, often radical, directions, with nuns blossoming into attractive modern décor and priests going to prison for burning draft records. As if to epitomize the change, it was not the fugitive Jesuit priest, Philip Berrigan, but the FBI agent arresting him who gave the order's battle cry: *"Ad majoram gloria Dei!"*

As for power, neither President Johnson nor President Nixon dared come out of the White House. Harry Truman striding down Park Avenue—so briskly that a reporter followed him on roller skates—is truly a nostalgic memory.

It is both an irony and a paradox that precisely at the time when trust and credibility in leaders are lowest, when people are angry as well as cynical, when we in leadership positions feel inhibited from exercising what power we have and the President himself seems morally powerless—this is precisely the time when the nation most needs people who can lead and who can transcend that vacuum. Unless we leaders do truly lead, it seems to me that our society is in very great danger, that a wave of still greater anarchy or even more violent crime could easily lead many bitter and fearful citizens to settle for a man on horseback—or in a tank—rather than anything that might resemble the democratic process.

The Requirements of Leadership

Given this perspective, what are the requirements, the skills, the competencies that we should seek in a leader—or that a leader himself should seek to develop?

With the enormous diversity of institutions, as well as their followers, there is no such thing as one type of leadership that is archetypal, ideal, for all. Almost every successful leader is, in a sense, lopsided, with one overriding gift that sometimes makes him also somewhat tunnel-visioned. He is like Isaiah Berlin's porcupine: "The fox knows many things, the hedgehog knows but one." His challenge is to develop his other, weaker sides.

Leadership is as much an art as a science, and the key tool is the person himself, his ability to learn what his strengths and skills are and to develop them to the hilt. The original Henry Ford could run the entire Ford

Motor Company by himself. That day is gone. Not only the sheer size, scale, and complexity of today's institutions but the incredible information overload that afflicts every chief executive makes this impossible.

Peter Drucker finds that there are some 45 key areas of decision making in today's typical large organization. The top man simply cannot provide direct oversight for all of it. Followers and leaders who think this is possible are trapped in a child's fantasy of absolute power and absolute dependence.

It seems to me that the leader, to function properly, simply must have what I have described as an "executive constellation." By no means an abdication of responsibility, it is a way of multiplying executive power through a realistic allocation of effort—particularly through temporary systems of assembling task forces for a particular assignment, then reassembling others for different ones.

The leader simply must have key assistants; but what kind, and with what perception of their functions, are vital questions. Earlier in this book I discussed at some length the doppelgänger phenomenon or syndrome that is duplicated in countless bureaucracies. Perhaps it is because I am a Cincinnatian that fellow air travelers have often commented to me how, for example, they can nearly always spot a P&G man on the plane. To be serious, however, the existence of doppelgängers is perfectly human, and up to a point understandable. The huge size of organizations and the overload make it impossible for the top leader to function effectively without congenial key assistants whom he feels he can trust and rely on.

But, in this "information economy," information itself is the chief lever of power—as it was also the chief target of the White House plumbers. Organizations are really information-processing systems, and the men who get power are the ones who learn how to filter the incredible flow of information into a meaningful pattern. That is why I have said that the *leader's biggest problem is to make sure that he gets all the needful information and that it has not been skewed by overeager doppelgängers to suit his perceived prejudices or hunches.*

In a burst of candor, the No. 3 man of one of our largest corporations, who had risen through the control and interpretation of data, once told me that he had spent virtually all the previous ten years proving his boss right even when he was wrong. However, that was a family dynasty; so possibly it should be no guide to others. Yet my own experience has taught me that what I say here is universal: The biggest problem of the president—any president—is getting the truth. This is equally true in industry, in academia, and in government.

What it boils down to is that the man at the top has to develop a process through which he not only gets the *right* information but also has at his disposal a system that can, with impunity, question his own assumptions—which may be prematurely or even wrongly formed. That's where the "scanners" and "sensors" become so important.

In almost every institution, you can find these men and women whom I have called, perhaps misleadingly, "marginal" or "borderline" people because their lives, contacts, and interests keep them at the margins, or boundaries, between the institution itself and the bigger, outside world. They can be, and should be, invaluable to a wise and prudent leader.

The irony and the tragedy of their position is that they are all too often marginal, and hence disposable, in the literal sense. They may get their heads chopped off for daring to tell the leader that what he thinks, as Kin Hubbard used to put it, "ain't necessarily so."

The bigger a bureaucracy, the greater is the danger that it may yield to a kind of incestuous inward-dwellingness, with middle management spending all its time writing self-justifying memos to each other and, as far as the outside world is concerned, scarcely knowing whether it is raining or is Thursday. The epitome of this proclivity was illustrated when the then head of General Motors, appearing before a Senate committee with all his retinue of advisers, was totally unprepared to discuss questions of automotive safety because he was totally unaware the Senators would raise them.

While attending a world conference of planners in Brussels, I stopped off in London to swap talk with Unilever executives. Unilever is well aware of this tone-deafness in middle management when it comes to knowing what's happening outside. Because it realizes that the longer a man is in middle management the more bad lessons he learns, it tries to spot first-rate talent very early, then rush the individual to the top as soon as possible. At the top, Unilever's reasoning goes, there is more opportunity for him to become more alert and perceptive, more cosmopolitan, more involved with the forces around the boundaries of the firm.

If, by and large, business people have fought the things in government policy that actually did them the most good and backed the things that would hurt them, it is largely because of this insular parochialism and lack of good information at the margins of their private world.

This danger emphasizes the value and importance of a periodic "moratorium" for executives whereby, as the Sloan Fellows do at MIT, they can cross-fertilize their latent creative instincts by swapping experiences with others and, above all, simply gaining the time and perspective for an intellectual "repotting."

Our institutions don't have enough "reflective structures" to take the time to examine, very seriously, their own operations. That's because they are so overloaded, so reactive to sheer immediate events, that they cannot ask the profoundest questions about where they really are and where they should be headed. I don't mean engaging in "long-range planning." I mean asking fundamental questions about the very purposes of the institution. Presidents don't do it. Boards of directors *should*, but are equally remiss.

Every manager has had the experience of listening to some outside counselor who, in five minutes, can have him saying, "My God, what wisdom!" about some problem whose solution was so perfectly obvious that no one inside the organization had thought of it—just as fish are the last to discover water. But management could have had the same insights if only it could have found the distance to achieve the outsider's perspective.

Management of Conflict

I have spoken of power or, rather, powerlessness. Leaders don't talk much about power any more. It's the last of our dirty little secrets. People now talk openly about sex, but they are still ambivalent about having and showing power.

Nevertheless, particularly at a time when *arribismo* makes consensus impossible, decisions have to be made. And, since they can't please all the caucuses, the best way to make them is to get *all* the information—including the negative advocacy—and then try to do what's right. You can heed Mark Twain's recommendation: "Always do what's right. It will gratify half of mankind and astound the other."

That brings me to the question of ethics. It is one of the prime ironies of our time that the heads of many corporations are being prosecuted for the very illegal political contributions that they were virtually blackjacked into giving by the former head of the very Justice Department now prosecuting them. But the fact remains that if they had not, long ago, acquiesced in an illegal practice because "everybody else was doing it," they would not have found themselves in this moral dilemma.

And that raises the question of the responsibility of directors. Did the directors, particularly the outside directors, of these corporations know about these illegal acts? If not, why not? That is a question that will, and should, be increasingly raised in the post-Watergate climate of corporate ethics. From here on in, any director who fails to learn of any intended illegality—*before* it is committed— may find himself being held legally culpable and financially responsible.

Above all, the task for today's leader is to create not only a climate of ethical probity but a climate in which it is possible for the people around him to grow and continue learning, in which contributions are prized and independence and autonomy are encouraged.

Forgive an educator if he puts in first place the leader's obligation to encourage the ability to learn. For more than 20 years, people in the Institute for Social Research, at the University of Michigan, have been trying to discover just what it is that gives a person satisfaction in a job. And they have finally concluded it is, above all, the opportunity and capacity to learn.

The task, then, of the leader is to lead.
To lead others, he must first of all know himself.

"MORTAL STAKES"

Leaders have a significant role in creating the state of mind that is the society. They can serve as symbols of the moral unity of the society. They can express the values that hold the society together. Most important, they can conceive and articulate goals that lift people out of their petty preoccupations, carry them above the conflicts that tear a society apart, and unite them in the pursuit of objectives worthy of their best efforts.

John W. Gardner, *No Easy Victories*

WHERE HAVE ALL
THE LEADERS GONE?

"Where have all the leaders gone?" They are, as a paraphrase of that haunting song could remind us, "long time passing."

All the leaders whom the young respect are dead. F.D.R., who could challenge a nation to rise above fear, is gone. Churchill, who could demand and get blood, sweat, and tears, is gone. Schweitzer, who from the jungles of Lambarene could inspire mankind with a reverence for life, is gone. Einstein, who could give us that sense of unity in infinity, of cosmic harmony, is gone. Gandhi, the Kennedys, Martin Luther King—all lie slain, as if to prove the mortal risk in telling us that we can be greater, better than we are.

The stage is littered with fallen leaders. A president reelected with the greatest plurality in history resigns in disgrace. The vice-president he twice chose as qualified to succeed him is driven from office as a common crook. Since 1973, the governments of all nine Common Market countries have changed hands. In nine recent months, nine more major governments have fallen. Shaky coalitions exist in Finland, Belgium, and Israel. Minority governments rule precariously in Britain, Denmark, and Sweden. Portugal overturned its fascist dictatorship and, as of this writing, has still not settled on a right-wing or left-wing dominated government. In Ethiopia, the King of Kings died a captive in his palace.

Where have all the leaders gone?

Those who remain—the successors, the survivors—are the Fords and Rockefellers who come to power without election, the struggling corporate chieftains, the university presidents, the city managers, the state governors. True leaders today are an endangered species. And why? Because of the whirl of events and circumstances beyond rational control.

There is a high turnover, an appalling mortality—whether occupational or actuarial—among leaders. In recent years the typical college president has lasted about four years. Men capable of leading institutions often refuse to accept such pressures, such risks. President Ford has had great difficulty getting the top men he wanted to accept Cabinet jobs. We see what James Reston of *The New York Times* calls "burnt-out cases," the debris of leaders. We see Peter Principle leaders rising to their final levels of incompetence. It has been said if a Martian were to demand, "Take me to your leader," Earthlings would not know where to take him. Administrative sclerosis around the world, in political office, in all administrative offices, breeds suspicion and distrust. A bumper sticker glimpsed in Massachusetts sums it up: "IMPEACH SOMEONE!"

We see people dropping out—not just college students but leaders of large institutions and businesses—to seek some Walden utopia without responsibility. We see more and more managers turning into Swiss gnomes who do not *lead* but attempt to barely manage.

A scientist at the University of Michigan has recently discussed what he considers to be the ten basic dangers to our society. First on his list of ten, and most significant, is the possibility of some kind of nuclear war or accident which would destroy the entire human race. The second basic challenge facing us is the prospect of a worldwide epidemic, disease, famine, or depression. The scientist's No. 3 in terms of the key problems which can bring about the destruction of society is *the quality of the management and leadership of our institutions.*

I think he's right. And, in effect, here we are: virtually without leaders. In the past year or so, we've seen four senior Congressional leaders, committee chairmen, deposed. In the new Congress, the new junior members have the power. Whether they can exercise it intelligently and responsibly is increasingly a question. The Congress used to get much more work done when there were some towering giants in those chambers: the "whales," as Lyndon Johnson called them—Rayburn, George, Vandenberg, Johnson himself. They were arrogant and sometimes oppressive, but nevertheless they managed to produce an aura that seemed to say things were getting done. Now there is scant attention to the basic issues of our times. The landscape of American politics is peculiarly flat and characterless.

In business, also, the landscape is flat. The giants that come to mind—Ford, Edison, Rockefeller, Morgan, Schwab, Sloan, Kettering—are no more. Nixon's business intimates were really outside the business establishment, entrepreneurs without widespread acceptance as leaders or spokesmen. And President Gerald Ford seems to get on best with the Washington *vice-presidents* of major corporations (a vice-president syndrome, as it were). Max Ways, in *Fortune* magazine, talks about the absence of business leaders in New York University's Hall of Fame. Of the 99 people selected, only 10 are business leaders. Education is more highly represented—Mark Hopkins, Nicholas Murray Butler, Mary Lyon, Horace Mann, Alice Freeman Palmer, Robert Hutchins, Booker T. Washington are among those honored.

But these giants in the field of education belong to yesterday's world. Today we see what appears to be a growing invisibility and blandness among educational leaders. Haverford College President Jack Coleman writes nostalgically about a vanished age: "Gone are the days when academic administrators offered leadership on a broad scale, whether it was on educational affairs or pressing public matters of the day." Is there now a college president who might, like Wilson, aspire to be President of the United States?

What about our cities, their management and leadership? My own city of Cincinnati hired one of the outstanding city managers in the nation—Bob Turner, a former president of the International City Managers Association. On March 1, 1975, after just three years on the job, he left—unable to realize the goals that he brought with him. (He is becoming a corporate executive, hoping for greater scope.) And in Detroit the first black mayor, Coleman Young, said to a jubilant crowd at his inauguration, "As of this moment, we're going to turn this city around." Less than a year later, Mayor Young in his "State of the City" address confessed that he had not been able to realize any of his goals, including the reduction of crime and the revitalization of industry in Detroit. It is as if the problems that people in leadership face are out of control.

There was a different time, when Carlisle could write about institutions as being the lengthened shadow of one man. And there was Pope Urban IV, whose retinue would greet him with a chant. "*Deus es. Deus es*," they would intone—to which he could reply, "It is somewhat strong, but really very pleasant." Leaders do not hear that kind of chant today. They have very few moments for hearing something adulatory or even merely pleasant.

A student at my university wrote me a letter after a talk he had heard me give. "Where," he asked, "is education to go in a society that becomes more and more dreamless each day?"

What shall I reply? What has dulled the image, not only of society, but of its leaders? We hunger for greatness, but what we find is, at best, efficient managers or, at worst, amoral gnomes lost in narrow orbits.

Why have we become a dreamless society? In the case of educational leaders, Haverford's Jack Coleman suggests that we have fallen into a "popularity trap." "We have asked too soon and too often whether our immediate constituents would like our programs and policies. Like other leaders of the day, we read polls."

It wasn't always that way. Not long ago a relative of M. Cary Thomas was describing that venerable woman's presidential years at Bryn Mawr College. An eager undergraduate asked, "Was she liked?" The answer was short: "I'm sure the question never crossed her mind."

Harry McPherson, a former counsel to President Lyndon Johnson, has some trenchant observations on leaders: "First, the media have overexposed public men, showing their feet and in some cases their whole bodies of clay. Television burns up new personalities quickly.

"Two, political, economic, and social changes which various leaders offered as remedies for the nation's ills are perceived as having failed or only partially succeeded."

Are leaders an endangered species?

The Problems and the Pressures

I have spent most of my life studying the best, the most rational, the most productive forms of organization and of leadership, whether of corporate, governmental, educational, or other institutions. Now, as I begin my fifth year of governing the nation's second largest urban multiversity —whose problems reflect in microcosm those of any complex organization—I can look back upon both accomplishments and failures.

I can compare what a specialist, a theorist, blithely believed *should* be done with what, in an imperfect world, *can* be done. I can compare what is desirable with what is possible. I know, as any leader of any organization—public, corporate, institutional—knows from experience, that the challenge is not for an omnipotent, omniscient "man on a white horse" but for a fallible, bewildered, often impotent individual to get one foot in the stirrup.

That is so because he confronts problems which may have no solutions or, at best, only proximate solutions. He confronts innumerable, diverse, and warring constituencies, whose separate goals and drives may be irreconcilable. The test, then, for any leader today is first to discover just *what* he does confront and then devise the best, the optimum, ways of making that reality potentially manageable.

Let me first try to set forth the conflicting demands— the turbulent, explosive environment—which make that task so difficult.

Foremost is *the loss of autonomy*. Time was when the leader could decide—period. A Henry Ford or a Carnegie could issue a ukase—and everyone would automatically obey. Their successors' hands are now tied in innumerable ways: by governmental requirements, by union rules, by the moral—and sometimes legal—pressures of organized consumers and environmentalists. As a supposed leader, I watch with envy the superior autonomy of the man mowing the university lawn. He is in complete control of the machine he rides, the total arbiter of which swath to cut where and when. I cannot match him.

The greatest problem facing today's institution is *the concatenation of external forces that impinge and impose upon it events outside the skin boundary of the organization.* Fifty years ago this external environment was fairly placid, like an ocean on a calm day, predictable, regular, not terribly eventful. Now that ocean is turbulent and highly interdependent and pivotal. In my own institution right now, the key people for me to reckon with are not only the students, the faculty, and my own management group, but people external to the university—the city manager, the city council members, the state legislature, the federal government, alumni, and parents. There is an incessant, dissonant clamor out there. And because the university is a brilliant example of an institution that has blunted and diffused its main purposes—through a proliferation of dependence on external patronage structures—its autonomy has declined to the point where our boundary system is like Swiss cheese. Because of these pressures, every leader must create, in effect, a department of "external affairs"—a secretary of state, as it were, to deal with external constituencies.

At the same time Henry Kissinger, a *real* secretary of state, finds foreign affairs thwarted by *internal constituencies* which undo his long, laborious, and precarious negotiations.

With this comes *a new movement of populism*—not the barn burners of the Grange days, not Bryan and his advocates of free silver against gold's "crown of thorns," but the fragmentation, the caucusization, of constituencies. On our campus, as I have mentioned in these pages, we have innumerable organized pressure groups—and the same phenomenon exists, more or less, in all large institutions. There is a loss of consensus, of community. We have a new form of politics in which people do not march on cities but march on particular bureaus or departments within our institutions.

We have become a *litigious society,* where individuals and groups more and more resort to the courts to determine issues which previously might have been settled privately. A hockey pro, injured in his sport, bypasses the institutional procedures to bring formal suit. My own university faces a suit from a woman, a black, for her loss of the administrative position I had thought she could fill. Even a law review has been sued—for rejecting an article.

In New Jersey, a federal judge has ordered 28 state senators to stand trial for violating the constitutional rights of the 29th member, a woman, by excluding her from their party caucus (they did so because she was "leaking" their deliberations to the press). In a Columbus, Ohio, test case, the Supreme Court ruled that secondary-school students may not be suspended, disciplinarily, without formal charges and a hearing—that the loss of a single day's education is a deprivation of property. A federal court in Washington has just awarded $10,000 to each of the thousands of May 1970 antiwar demonstrators who it found had been illegally arrested and confined. Without questioning the merits of any particular case, the overriding fact is clear that the hands of all administrators are increasingly tied by real or potential legal issues. I find I must consult our lawyers even over small, trivial decisions.

With the neopopulism comes the phenomenon which I have described as *arribismo*. The U.S. brand of *arribismo* distinguishes all those diverse Americans who are trying to find themselves along race lines, sex lines, ethnic lines, even age lines—all at different stages of their social identity and their economic and political power.

And the neopopulism and the *arribismo* are accompanied by a related development that we might call the *psychology of entitlement*. It asserts one's right to things that one might not deserve through merit or achievement, simply because one's whole group has been deprived—by racism or whatever—from normal enjoyment of them. It demands *x* number of jobs regardless of individual qualifications.

These pressure groups are not united but fragmented. They go their *separate and often conflicting ways*. It is they who are telling us that the old dream of the melting pot, of assimilation, does not work. They have never been *beyond* the melting pot; rather, they have been *behind* it. They say, "Forget about your mainstream. We just want to be *us*"—blacks, homosexuals, Chicanos, women's libbers, or Menominee Indians seizing an empty Catholic monastery.

Meanwhile, the country is trying to cope with the *Roosevelt legacy*, the post-Depression development in the public sector of those areas of welfare, social service, and education that the private sector was unwilling or unable to handle. As Lord Keynes wrote: "Progress lies in the growth and the recognition of semi-autonomous bodies within the states. Large business corporations, when they have reached a certain age and size, approximate the status of public corporations rather than that of the individualistic private enterprise." The Keynesian prophecy is upon us.

When David Rockefeller goes to London, he is greeted as if he were a chief of state (and some of his empires are bigger than many states). But, in addition to the semi-autonomous, often global corporations, rivaling governments, which Lord Keynes envisioned, we also have public-sector institutions which he could scarcely have imagined. The largest employment sector of our society, which is growing at the fastest rate, is local and state government. *Higher education, which less than 20 years ago was 50 percent private and 50 percent public, is now about 85 percent public and is expected to be 90 percent public by 1980.*

And, *where a century ago 90 percent of all Americans were self-employed, today 90 percent now work in what can be called bureaucracies.* They are members of some kind of corporate family. They might be called "juristic" persons; that is, they work within the sovereignty of a legal entity called a corporation or bureaucracy. Juristic persons do not control their own actions; hence they cannot place the same faith in each other that they might if they were self-employed.

And along with the growth of public-sector institutions, we have seen its handmaiden—a *cat's cradle of regulations which tend to restrict or reduce the institution's autonomy in decision making.* What we now have is a situation where many of the decisions being made by any major organization, public or private, have to do with factors that are partly outside the control, and definitely outside the governing perimeter, of the organization itself.

To take just one example, the university, the Buckley Amendment makes all records available to students and parents. It obviously changes every aspect of information sharing and the way recommendations are written about students.

Leaders are becoming an endangered species, also, because *the external forces and the internal constituents,
themselves with diverse expectations and demands and desires, isolate the man at the top* as the sole "boundary" person trying somehow to negotiate between them. Growing
tension, conflict, goal divergence develop between the internal and external demands. In my own city a Kroger's or
a P&G must consider both external as well as internal
problems, whether nitrates or price labeling. Or take the
effects of "affirmative action" on what used to be autonomous decisions made by the organization. The overload of
these demands from within and without the institution is
enormous.

*Within the community, we have not only a loss of con-
sensus over basic values, we have as well a polarization. We
have not a consensus but a dissensus.*

Finally, consider the change of values among the young,
as reflected in the surveys done recently by Yankelovich.
We've gone from concern for *quantity*—that is, *more*—toward considerations of *quality*—that is, *better*. The old culture focused on the concept of *independence*, whereas the
new culture moves toward the concept of *interdependence*
of nations, institutions, individuals, all natural species. What
youth is saying is that we need a new "declaration of interdependence." That we must move from conquest of nature
toward living in harmony with it, from competition toward
cooperation, from doing and planning toward being, from
the primacy of technology toward considerations of social
justice and equity, from the dictates of organizational convenience toward the aspirations of self-realization and learning, from authoritarianism and dogmatism toward more
participation, from uniformity and centralization toward
diversity and pluralism, from the concept of work as hard

and unavoidable, from life as nasty, brutish, and short toward work as purpose and self-fulfilment, a recognition of leisure as a valid activity in itself.

The people who are joining our organizations and institutions today are those who seek, who represent, the latter part of each of those dichotomies. They are the New Culture.

Why "Leaders" Don't "Lead"

These, then, are the problems of leadership today. We have the new and important emergence of a Roosevelt-Keynes revolution, new politics, new dependencies, new constituencies, new values. The consequence of these pressures is a loss of the institution's autonomy to determine its own destiny.

So why are "leaders" not "leading"?

One reason, I fear, is that many of us don't have the faintest concept of what leadership is all about. Leading does not mean managing; the difference between the two is crucial. There are many institutions I know that are very well *managed* and very poorly *led*. They may excel in the ability to handle all the routine inputs each day, yet they may never ask whether the routine should be preserved at all.

As I noted earlier, frequently my most enthusiastic deputies unwittingly do their best to keep me from working any fundamental change in the institution. I think all of us find that acting on routine problems, just because they are the easiest, often blocks us from getting involved in the bigger ones.

In recent years I have talked to many new presidents of widely ranging enterprises. Almost every one of them feels that the biggest mistake he made at the start was to *take on too much*, as if proving oneself depended on providing instant solutions and success was dependent on immediate achievement. The instant solutions often led to *pseudo-solutions* for problems not fully analyzed. People follow the old army game. They do not want to take responsibility for, or bear the consequences of, decisions that they should properly make. Everybody tries to dump those "wet babies" on the boss's desk—defenseless and unequipped as he is.

Today's leader is often baffled or frustrated by a new kind of politics, which arises from significant interaction with various governmental agencies, relevant laws and regulations, the courts, the media, the consumers, and so on. It is the politics of maintaining institutional "inner-directedness" and mastery in times of rapid change. Many institution leaders do not want to face up to the need for politicking. Not long ago, when the director of the New York Health Corporation resigned, he declared, "I already see indications of the corporation and its cause being made a political football in the current campaign. I'm not a politician. I do not wish to become involved in the political issues here." And yet, in a previous article, he had said that he found himself "at the center of a series of ferocious struggles for money, power, and jobs among the combatants, political leaders, labor leaders, minority groups, medical militants, medical-school deans, doctors and nurses, and many of his own administrative subordinates." The corporation he headed has an $800 million budget and is responsible for capital construction of more than $1 billion; it employs 40,000 people, including 7,500 doctors and almost 15,000 nurses and nurse's aides. It embraces 19 hospitals with 15,000 beds and numerous outpatient clinics and emergency rooms that treat 2,000,000 New Yorkers a year. And he's *surprised* that he's into politics—and doesn't like it!

When our own university could admit only 187 medical-school applicants out of 8,000, we immediately angered some 23,000 would-be constituents—24,000 parents and applicants minus the successful applicants and their parents, who were pleased. Those who were unhappy immediately brought pressure on councilmen and legislators. What resulted was proposals to legislate restrictions on our autonomy—for example, to bar out-of-state students. We could resent and oppose that, and we did. But we should not have been surprised by it. We should have known that such decisions automatically *become* political.

The high turnover and the appalling mortality among leaders remain. The landscape continues flat. The problems seem insoluble—to the degree that we are becoming a dreamless society. Now we hear that butterflies are to be listed as a threatened species. Can we allow leaders to go the same route?

THE SHAPE
OF THE FUTURE

Yes, the great leaders are gone, but the people—particularly the young—hunger for new ones of the same stature. And there is a spiritual thirst despite the falling-off of church attendance and membership. The thousands turning to inward-dwelling mysticism make their own dreams in the dreamless society.

There is, above all, a craving for that integrity and simplicity which mark the truly great—a Lincoln, an Einstein, a Holmes, a Schweitzer.

To repeat: *It is the paradox of our times that precisely when the trust and credibility of leaders are at their lowest, when the beleaguered survivors in leadership positions feel unable to summon up the vestiges of power left to them, we most need people who can lead.* The alternative, it seems to me, is a heightening of our present danger, an increase in the sort of organizational paralysis that is already endemic in our institutions, a failure of nerve that could pave the way for a new and perhaps more insidious type of demagogue.

Given this gloomy perspective, let's examine the requirements of genuine leadership in such a complex and confusing era. Harlan Cleveland, rewording Wilson, calls today's large organizations "a jungle of close decisions openly arrived at." That's a valid description. The organization of today is big, complex, and surrounded by an active, incessant environment which is becoming more influential and dominant in the kinds of decisions that affect the institution. In a sense, organizations have a difficult time, just as individuals do, in becoming self-determining.

But institutions are going to become *bigger* and *more complex, more inclusive* than ever before. This may sadden both the reactionary and the radical who are nostalgic for the "ma and pa" corner grocery or the one-room schoolhouse. However, the power and pervasiveness of new technologies will require ever more intricate systems, more expensive systems, and more specialists involved in decision making.

Therefore, we can expect that decision making will become an increasingly involved process of multilateral brokerage, a brokerage that will include people both *within* the organization and *outside* the organization. And, more and more, decisions will be public in the sense that they affect people who intend to be heard, especially if a decision doesn't suit them. So more and more constituencies will have to be brought in, given a chance to voice their opinions. Management will have to take into account ethnic and other groups that they have never before had to consider except through market research.

Moreover, today's leader must consider the growing role of the fourth estate, the media, as the fourth arm of government. The media will be used both by those who favor, but even more by those who oppose, particular decisions. The decisions involved will affect more and more people. Already a product cannot be distributed in many retail areas unless various consumer groups and organizations are consulted. Nor can administrators make decisions on mass transit, on pollution, on whether to build fewer highways or more railways without involving the appropriate constituents. The fact is that the concept of "movers and shakers"—a clearly defined elite who determine the major decisions—is an outdated notion. They are as much the shaken—the "shook"—as they are the shakers.

The bigger the problem to be tackled, the more power will be diffused and the more people there will be who exercise it. Decisions are increasingly difficult and specialized; they affect more, and different kinds of, constituencies.

We're moving toward what the Russians call "collective leadership." We already see analogies of this in some of our most successful corporate institutions—Union Carbide, for example—where executive constellations or task forces are created for specific purposes. In light of Drucker's estimate that all large institutions have at least 45 core functions or goals, the notion of *one-man* leadership has to be seriously questioned. I would wager that we will see more and more collective leadership in all institutions. If President Ford is working much more in tandem, much more closely, with his Vice-President than have previous Presidents, it is because he recognizes that the managerial complexities of running such a huge establishment as our federal government require a stronger executive framework. It is significant that Ford turned over to Rockefeller deputies the Domestic Council powers previously held by Ehrlichman as Nixon's No. 2 aide.

Such changes will lead to a lot of frustration about who's on the team and who isn't, who's in charge and who isn't. The name of the game will be *ambiguity*, and people had damn well better get used to it and learn how to cope with it. There will be more politicization, new kinds of politics, new organizational politics. There will be more constituencies, more voices, more concerns, more caucuses, more regulations, more capricious and unpredictable litigation. And there will be—in fact, there is already—a blurring of the traditional line between public and private sectors. There will be elements of each in the other.

These are the kinds of characteristics that mark the organizations we are now living in. My own view is that they will become more pronounced, more visible, in the years ahead; that it is incumbent upon all of us—in particular, those who aspire to positions of responsibility—to understand them, to cope with them, and to learn how to be masters of our own fate in a wholly different kind of organizational environment.

All this augurs more frustration for the followers as well as the leaders. Certainly more than ever before it is mandatory that there be better, deeper understanding between the leaders and the led. Else neither will be leading or being led.

How Managers Can Lead

Again, the first requirement for genuine leadership performance is that leaders at every level must *lead*, not just manage.

Let me emphasize once more how strongly I believe that any manager's first and foremost priority is to *create around him some kind of executive team*, what I have termed a "constellation," to help direct and run the office of the leader. They needn't—indeed, they mustn't—be "little leaders" or carbon copies of one another, but they must be compatible, able to work as a team, knowledgeable and competent within their areas of specialization, and very serious about the idea of a "president's office" or "executive constellation" and its importance.

There's an interesting, easy group exercise I use which goes like this: We try, on one axis of a blackboard, to identify what a particular office must or should do—what its goals, tasks, objectives are, both short-term and long-term. Then we ask each individual what it is that he or she wants to do, is motivated to do, aspires to do. And then, finally, we look at competence. How competent are various individuals to perform those tasks? What I strive for, but never fully succeed in doing, is to create a fit, a triangulation, between competence and capacity and aspiration— what each person wants to do—and what *needs* to be done in each particular job.

The leader, at every level, must be partly a conceptualist, something more than just an "idea man." By that I mean someone with a kind of entrepreneurial vision, a sense of perspective, and, most of all, the time to spend thinking about the forces that will affect the destiny of that person's shop or that institution.

In this connection a story comes to my mind: A king returned to his capital, followed by his victorious army. The band played; and the king's horse, the army, the people all moved in step with the rhythm. The king, amazed, contemplated the power of music. Suddenly he noticed a man who was walking out of step and slowly falling behind. Deeply impressed, the monarch sent for the man and told him, "I never saw a man as strong as you are. The music has enthralled everybody except you. Where do you get the strength to resist it?" The man answered, "I was pondering, and that gave me the strength."

That old story is relevant to the point I want to make. Almost all leaders complain about getting involved, or overly involved, in routine (turning off the lights, the day-to-day operations). Given the overload on all of us, it's understandable. But I don't think this is any excuse for not realizing that one of the main functions of every leader, every manager, is to maintain his sense of perspective, to know how to ask the right questions, to be a conceptualist, to be able to look ahead so that an organization or part of that organization can make the right decisions for the future. It is not only generals who are always fighting the last war.

The leader must create for his institution clear-cut and measurable goals, based on advice from all its many constituencies. He must be allowed to proceed toward those goals without being crippled by bureaucratic machinery and routine that sap his strength, energy, and initiative. He must be allowed to take risks, to embrace error, to use his creativity to the hilt, and encourage others in the institution to use theirs. This cannot be done without the leader's taking on a role of studied detachment, occasionally declaring a "time out" moratorium, or developing some "reflective structure" where he can ponder, where personal and organizational strength can be regained, and where institutional goals can become vital and adaptive.

Because we live in an information economy and information itself is one of the chief levers of power, one of the leader's top-priority responsibilities is to make sure that he gets all the valid information he needs and make sure, difficult as it is, that the information he gets has not been distorted by those anxious, well-meaning doppelgängers who present material to suit what they consider to be his prejudices or hunches. He must learn to identify and utilize the marginal, borderline "sensors" and "scanners" in the organization—people whose sense of discrepancy enables them to detect variances between the achievements of the organization and its aspirations, people who have the future in their bones, people who (without low-level grumbling and bellyaching) can spot dissatisfaction in themselves and others and who long for greater achievement. Helpful as they can and should be to a wise leader, their problem is that so often the news they bring is bad, or it contradicts the conventional wisdom of the prevalent culture inside the organization, and they find their services dispensed with.

Not only top management but middle management may be victimized by overprotection and isolation. In the case of middle management, the basic difficulty is the length of time that too many people spend going up the hierarchical ladder. This is inevitably a period of their lives during which they are enclosed by the norms and beliefs and values that are peculiar to middle management. They work themselves up, but they are subject in the process to too much corseting and insularity. When they get to the top, a whole new array of forces—environmental, political, economic, financial—confronts them in the form of things they have never considered.

For example, people who come up through the financial end of an institution are bookkeepers by instinct and training. They move up through the organization, learning rigid methods and procedures, the latest bookkeeping techniques, security measures, sophisticated management controls. But, at the very top, the vice-president in charge of finance is really involved in legitimate gambling and risk taking; nothing in his previous experience as a bookkeeper, an accountant, or a steward over other people's money is in any way preparation for that high-level role. Small wonder that, frequently, people get to the top who are really unprepared for top responsibilities.

Organizations should be transitive. That is, being in Job A should prepare you for Job B; being in Job B should prepare you for Job C. Often management tends to keep people in particular jobs so long that they *overlearn* the competencies in Job B before they get into Job C. In the case of the financial or bookkeeping trajectory, we see an organization and a career line being nontransitive. I suspect this is really the core reason for the so-called Peter Principle, which states that people are promoted to their ultimate level of incompetence. It isn't that people just get lazy and obsolete. The fact is that they can be in a job and get promoted to another job for which they have absolutely no preparation, no training, no background. So we have unprepared people in a highly turbulent environment. It is this situation that often leads to businesses opting for government policies that will be to their disadvantage and, at other times, fighting policies which would be to their advantage.

At MIT's Sloan School of Management and Harvard's Graduate School of Business Administration, executives on leave from responsible positions make the most of their "time out." The Sloan Fellows used to say that during their year at MIT they learned a lot about computer sciences, about industrial dynamics, and about the human side of enterprise. To me, however, as one who watched them, it seemed that their greatest gain was not from their course work, although indeed they did get a lot from that. It was simply the fact that they and their families had a year away from it all, with other executives in similar positions, and so gained a new perspective, a kind of detachment. The German word for "retreat"—zurücktreten—

means literally to take a step backward. It also has the added meaning of gaining perspective, so as not to be, as Gertrude Stein said, "too immediate to be immediate."

It is truly unfortunate that our institutions don't build in reflective structures where we can take time out to examine ourselves and our operations in a very serious way; that we are too overloaded, too reactive to sheer, immediate events to ask the *big* questions—the ones that concern *the very purposes of the institution.* All of us are capable of having the same fresh insights that highly paid consultants have—if only we could find the historical distance to achieve an outsider's new perspective.

The Leader as Social Architect

At whatever level, a manager must be a social architect vitally concerned with the environment of work, with what the social scientists call the "culture" of work. The elements are hard to discern, impossible to touch, but so terribly important in their impact on the way people act; that is, the set of values which guide their decision making and their behavior.

The culture of work can be observed in terms of its effects. For example, in some companies there is a norm or belief or value system which, overtly or tacitly, *tends to reduce risk taking,* tends to make people check things out 15 times, tends to have executives keep what Chris Argyris refers to as JIC files—"just in case" the boss calls you and asks for some forgotten piece of information which dates back years and years.

Then, too, the culture of work can be observed in terms of the kinds of relationships that exist among people. How close can you move to others? What are the norms and rules regarding intimacy, distance between people? How much control are people subjected to? How much independence are they allowed? How much support do they give each other?

Lots of things go into producing a culture—the style of leadership, the particular technology of the institution, its peculiar history, and so on. The leader must understand his organization's social architecture, the climate and culture within which he works. Indeed, he himself can have some part in creating and maintaining these or, contrariwise, debilitating them.

Social architecture is important because more and more people joining the workplace are looking for careers that not only make money but make sense and have meaning. More and more people are selecting jobs that will not only further their professional or career goals but will also give them a fuller life.

The nationwide survey by Yankelovich Associates which I mentioned earlier reveals that there is a blurring or diminishing of differences among the young—individuals aged 18 to 26—with regard to basic lifestyles, goals, and career aspirations. *The noncollege youth and the college student now think alike.* An earlier survey, made in the late 1960s of student disruptions, showed that there was no "generation gap," that upper-middle-class white students had very little disagreement with their parents. The same thing was true among the blue-collar, working population —there wasn't very much difference between the hard-hats and their mothers and fathers. However, while there was no generation gap, the Yankelovich group found there *was* a difference based on class and, to some extent, ethnic background.

The newest survey shows that the difference *between*

classes has practically evaporated and is no longer statistically significant. It isn't just the Scarsdale Maoist, it isn't just the upper-middle-class comfortable folk, it is now the noncollege workers, the union members, who share the same values as the college kids. And, while you can't make too many generalizations on the basis of hair length, just take a look at your local policemen—just take a look at the workers on the local assembly line—and see if you can detect a difference in dress, manner, and aspirations from those in college.

That means that we're going to have to create institutions in which people can feel the possibility of growing and continuing to learn, where contributions are prized, where independence and autonomy are encouraged. What is it that workers at the Institute for Social Research, coordinated by Dr. Robert Kahn, have discovered after trying for two decades to identify just what gives one satisfaction in one's job? They have concluded that it is above all *the opportunity and capacity to learn*. When that is no longer present, job satisfaction wavers and declines. The most progressive unions are aware of this—they are now emphasizing those areas of the work life that have to do with *learning*, with the *quality* of the work, with the opportunities for advancement through education. So leaders, in their role as social architects, have to create those cultures and structures that facilitate these goals. Not just in the young. Their elders have goals too—they've just been somewhat more reticent about expressing them.

A social architect must also deal with ethics. No one in a position of responsibility and authority, in whatever type of organization, can any longer be ignorant of what is done in its name. The culture of an organization will dictate and govern its honesty and probity.

Consider the culture of science. Scientists are no more honest in their personal behavior than others. But it is interesting that there have been few cases of scientists faking their data or fudging reality. The reason is that the *norm* of science has within it corrective mechanisms in the replication of experiments. Even more important is the fact that a scientist reports data *publicly*.

It would be very easy to fake data. Recently there have been two cases where that was done. But it is remarkable how few there are, given the magnitude of the research going on. So I disagree with those who believe that we need a written ethical code. A written ethical code can never be comprehensive enough or subtle enough to be a satisfactory guide to personal behavior. The answer to ethical problems lies in the very warp and woof of institutional culture. It is to be seen in those things that we tacitly allow and disallow. The leader can establish a new ethic by refusing to go along with the debasement of ethics.

The Management of Differences

There are some areas in which the leader has to be the final arbiter. As a former organizational consultant, and now as one who presides over a large institution, I am convinced that how an organization deals with conflict is probably the best clue to its proper functioning. Organizations have different patterns, different mechanisms, for coping with conflict.

In a broad sense we look at, see, touch conflict almost every day. Talk to the head of a sales department in a major corporation about his attitudes toward, let's say, engineering or production. Talk to certain staff members about their perceptions of line personnel—and vice versa. In some organizations intergroup conflict resembles a form of urban guerrilla warfare. The "others" are not even part of the species; they're a sort of a pseudo-species that exists in some funny alien tribe they would like to vanquish. In fact, it seems at times as if the main objective is to destroy the competitors within the organization rather than the competitors without. The "enemy" is not across the street but across the hall. That's true in every organization and institution. If it weren't, I wouldn't believe that there could be an *effective* organization.

The problem is, how do we contain the conflict (because it *is* inevitable), and how do we make it creative and useful? How do we really get those competitive energies into constructive and creative channels?

There are two reasons for the kinds of conflict that one sees most in organizations. The simplest is information. *Y* has information that *A* doesn't have. It gets exciting when, as often happens, *A* and *Y* may have information which is diametrically opposite. It's not too difficult to deal with informational discrepancies, although quite often that's the basis for what grows into a more virulent kind of conflict.

Another reason for conflict is the perceptual apparatus —people's varying perceptions. When I was a consultant with the State Department, we did some interesting exercises while trying to develop more understanding about the conflicts between the administrative and the career-ambassador types. The one viewed the other as basically an effete Princeton or Ivy League type—"He can't start his car, so how can he run an embassy?" And the ambassadors had what was probably a more benign contempt and a much more clever way of talking about the administrators, ignoring the fact that some of them were very powerful men and some had been heads of large corporations.

Perceptual differences, in short, are not merely based on competition over scarce resources, on differing backgrounds, or disparate ages. Where you are determines how you see things, just as where you sit determines where you stand. So it is that our various roles are involved in the conflicts existing in organizations.

How do we deal with these conflicts? Usually badly! By definition, a problem is something which *persists;* and the tactics and strategies, usually not conscious policies, which are applied in the effort to solve it tend at best to put the problem or conflict under the rug. What we often see is a persistent tendency for leaders to surround themselves with yes men despite the fact that they will always say, "I don't *want* yes men." We find a tendency to emphasize loyalty and cooperation in a way that makes disagreement seem equivalent to disloyalty and rebellion, if not sedition. We find leaders glossing over serious differences in order to maintain a false appearance of harmony and teamwork; accepting ambiguous, mushy solutions of differences which permit the conflicting parties to arrive at dissimilar interpretations (actually they usually know better); or exploiting differences to strengthen their personal influence while, at the same time, weakening the position of others.

There are, fortunately, ways of really coping with conflict. In fact, there is a choice of ways, and one of the prime responsibilities of the leader is to exercise that choice. When leaders are ineffective, it's often because they tend to reply in identical, static ways to problems that differ greatly. They tend to be repetitive rather than flexible. They are not exercising the choice available to them. Yet organizations have infinite opportunities for coping effectively with conflict and making it a creative source of energy.

What I see most of all is avoidance, the denial of conflict. For, if conflict is denied, it is avoided. It sticks out at a consultant coming in. To be sure, avoidance sometimes is wise. There are times not to fight, and there are times to keep conflict somewhat at bay. Along with avoidance goes repression, which is somewhat sterner (a parental version is "We won't talk about that!"). Repression of differences or conflict is punitive. It's saying that anybody who wants to face up to conflicts or differences will be punished, and we certainly will never reward the open expression of differences. People learn that; it's part of the culture again.

Another tactic, often used by a type of organizational leader that we occasionally see glorified in movies and novels, has to do with pitting two or more deputies in a kind of gladiatorial combat. I have heard executives say, "Well, I'm just going to see what old Joe and old Bill do to one another for the next year or two," which is, I suppose, a form of legitimate genocide. But I cannot think of many situations where that would be an effective way of dealing with differences and conflicts.

All too infrequently do executives try to make conflict creative. They seldom look on conflicts and differences with managerial objectivity and view them as educational opportunities. Yet I see a segment of any manager's or leader's role as being educational. Quite often we can learn from differences—and I'm not talking about just learning the other point of view. Almost always, if we really analyze differences and conflicts, the process of doing so will identify a significant problem that the organization has not yet learned how to handle.

How, specifically, do we convert conflicts and differences into potential opportunities for better problem solving? It goes without saying that we must welcome the existence of differences; after all, they're going to be there whether we like it or not. Beyond that, we must try to create approaches which we can learn from.

Learning from conflict is based on the assumption that the leader will have the proper managerial objectivity, the necessary perspective and judgment. The people reporting to him will all have their own particular areas of competence, orientations, vested interests, blind spots based on role and perceptions. Somehow or other the manager has to have the ecumenical view and the impartiality that should go with it.

The Challenges of the Times

It's interesting to ask, "Just what is it that leaders in fact *do* do at the present time?" without putting any evaluation on it. What do we know descriptively about the behavior of leaders?

Only recently Henry Mintzberg made a study * to try to categorize the behavioral patterns of leaders. He found eight areas of prime importance:

1. Peer skills—the ability to establish and maintain a network of contacts with equals.
2. Leadership skills—the ability to deal with subordinates and the kinds of complications that are created by power, authority, and dependence.
3. Conflict-resolution skills—the ability to mediate conflict, to handle disturbances under psychological stress.
4. Information-processing skills—the ability to build networks, extract and validate information, and disseminate information effectively.

* *The Nature of Managerial Work.* Harper & Row, 1973.

THE SHAPE OF THE FUTURE

5. Skills in *unstructured* decision making—the ability to find problems and solutions when alternatives, information, and objectives are ambiguous.
6. Resource-allocation skills—the ability to decide among alternative uses of time and other scarce organizational resources.
7. Entrepreneurial skills—the ability to take sensible risks and implement innovations.
8. Skills of introspection—the ability to understand the position of a leader and his impact on the organization.

I think that is a splendid list. From my own experience as a leader, and from talking with other executives and, as a consultant, observing other leaders at work, I believe these pretty well summarize the basic skills leaders need.

But there's more than that—an *x* factor that is quintessential for leadership. Leaders have to *define* the issues, not aggravate the problems. They have to clarify the problems, not exploit them. In effect, leaders are essentially educators. Our great political leaders—such as Jefferson, Lincoln, and Wilson—have been men who tried to educate people about both the problems facing the country and the deeper underlying issues. They also sought to develop solutions to those problems.

A leader who responds to unemployment by attacking shiftlessness is not likely to inspire confidence. And what we see quite often is the problem being left as a problem rather than the underlying issue being uncovered and a possible solution arrived at. Martin Luther King, Jr. provided perspective, inside illumination, and understanding for the black people of this country. We sorely need leadership that can do this for our entire nation. Lyndon

Johnson once said, "Get your head above the grass." And, in the same farmyard language, someone else once said that any rooster who sticks his head above the grass will get a rock thrown at it. That's true, but it's exactly where a leader's head belongs.

John Gardner tells us that the best-kept secret in America today is the need of people to believe and to dedicate themselves to purposes that are worthy and that are bigger than they are. I am certain that the need to believe—fidelity to an idea, an ideal—is necessary for our mental health. Erik Erikson, the distinguished psychiatrist, suggests that maturity cannot be reached until there is fidelity to an ideal, a value, a belief. The good leader understands and develops ideas and issues that resonate with this need to believe, this need to dedicate oneself, this need to give something to a cause greater than oneself. The Peace Corps tapped that need—and we saw remarkable people, young and old, flock forth to work for it. We need, in Frost's lapidary phrase, to "work and play for mortal stakes."

The leader must also recognize imperfection and, at the same time, retain a sense of optimism and of hope. A study of the effective psychotherapist once showed that his particular orientation, or the school from which he came, had little to do with his effectiveness. *The common chord among successful therapists had to do with whether they had hope in their ability to solve a problem, in their ability to help someone.* Similarly, in a study of schoolteachers, it turned out that when they held high expectations for their students, *that alone was sufficient to cause an increase of 25 points in the students' I.Q. scores.* When the teachers seemed to have low expectations or hopes, the scores had no significant difference.

What qualities do all these challenges I have noted demand from new leaders? After at least 50 years of research and theorizing, we can say only one thing with any confidence: There are no provable generalizations about leadership.

That indefinable quality called "charisma" is sometimes mentioned. But there are charismatic people who do *not* become leaders, and there are noncharismatic people who do. Herbert Hoover, Clement Atlee, and Golda Meir come to mind as leaders who have lacked charisma.

There are low-energy leaders and high-energy leaders. There are attractive and unattractive leaders. But all the accumulated research in personal psychology suggests there is not one single trait or characteristic that would have any value in predicting leadership potentialities. None—*not even intelligence.*

It seems to me the big test for any new leader will be whether or not he can—by identifying with the process of change—ride or even direct it and, by so doing, build new strengths in the process. By identifying with change he will find himself changing, growing.

I remember an old Talmudic story. An oriental king, who had heard that Moses was a kindly, generous, and bold leader, had a portrait of Moses brought to him. He called his astrologers and phrenologists together to examine it. Looking at it carefully, they told the king that Moses was a cruel, greedy, craven, self-seeking man. Puzzled, the king went to visit Moses. On meeting him, he saw that Moses was good: "My phrenologists and astrologers were wrong," he said. But Moses disagreed: "Your phrenologists and astrologers were right. They saw what I was made of; but what they couldn't tell you was that I struggled against all that and so became what I am."

Like Moses, the leader who does learn to "cope," to

direct change, may find himself or herself quite a different person some years hence. For the task of the leader is to lead, and to lead others he must first of all know himself.

The ultimate test of the leader is the wise use of power. I find myself returning over and over to those words of Sophocles in *Antigone:* "But hard it is to learn the mind of any mortal, or the heart, till he be tried in chief authority. Power shows the man."

Power, leadership, authority have very recently shown all too clearly the man, the men, who could not use it wisely or properly. If the landscape is littered with those who were tried and found wanting, it is for us to profit from their example, so that the endangered species may survive.

As for the best leaders, the people do not notice their existence. The next best, the people honor and praise. The next, the people fear; and the next, the people hate. . . .

When the best leader's work is done, the people say, "We did it ourselves."

Robert Townsend, Up the Organization

ACKNOWLEDGMENTS

"One Job, One Year, One Life" is based on a brief review of Ken Metzler's *Confrontation: The Destruction of a College President* (Nash, 1973), published in the September 19, 1973, issue of *Change Magazine*.

"The Unconscious Conspiracy—and How to Confound It" originally appeared in the January 1973 issue of the *Saturday Review of Education* under the title "View from the Top." It is used here with the publisher's permission.

"Resignation for Principle" first appeared under the title "When to Resign" in *Esquire* for June 1972 and is reprinted here by permission. It was written in collaboration with Patricia Ward Biederman. Copyright 1972 Esquire, Inc.

"Surviving the Revolution of Consciousness" ("How to Survive in a Revolution") originally was published in the March 1970 issue (No. 11) of *Innovation*, copyright © 1970 by Technology Communication, Inc. Reprinted by permission of Executive Video-Forum, Inc. New York.

"A Little Lower than the Angels" was an address delivered at the Mount Washington Presbyterian Church, Cincinnati, Ohio, on December 9, 1973.

"People, Change, and the Adaptive Process" was originally entitled "Everything You Always Wanted to Know About Change (but were afraid to ask)." It is reprinted, with permission, from *ENVIRONMENT/Planning and Design*. Summer 1971. Copyright 1971 Herman Miller, Inc.

"Perils of the Bureaucratic Way." A much-condensed version of this chapter appeared as the "My Turn" column of September 17, 1973, in *Newsweek*.

"Meet Me in Macy's Window" first appeared in the October 1975 issue of *Harvard Magazine*.

"Leader Power in an Explosive Environment" was a talk before the 1973 Annual Management Conference of the Cincinnati Chamber of Commerce on October 22, 1973. It was then entitled "Leadership in the Age of Arribismo."